AF327459

"THE ETERNAL UNIVERSE"

By

Harold W.G. Allen

By the same author:
Ye Shall Know the Truth
The Edge of The Universe
Higher Perspective

THE ETERNAL UNIVERSE

DEDICATION

It is a feature of our earthly existence that one may strive a lifetime in a vain quest for knowledge; while yet another may be so fortunate as to inherit vital information in the form of history and tradition. Scientific advances of the present generation alone have given us much precious insight that was denied to many inquisitive minds of the past. Only in a limited sense, therefore, may this work be considered a personal interpretation of our mysterious universe. Indeed, it was made possible solely through the unselfish contributions of others, some of whom received not even the satisfaction of knowing the real worth of their discoveries.

Accordingly, it is to the memory of those who have sought in vain, to those that today and in the future are genuine in their search for Truth, that this book is hereby dedicated.

THE ETERNAL UNIVERSE

PREFACE

A constant threat to scientific progress is the sin of prejudice - a trait from which no researcher can be said to be completely immune. Unfortunately, it is all too easy for a budding professional to subscribe to popular ideas, rather than risk censure from one's colleagues. But the measure of a true scientist lies in the ability to examine all possibilities - even if it means questioning the validity of "established" precepts! Indeed, history has clearly revealed many instances where a popular viewpoint was later conceded to be in error.

At the frontiers of astronomical inquiry, where interpretation is often a matter of opinion, the temptation to jump to hasty conclusions is frequently very strong, as man endeavors to formulate some picture of a highly complex and mysterious universe. Accordingly, a number of vital concepts (such as the Big Bang model of creation) have come to be looked upon by many as actual fact instead of mere hypothesis. The time may well be ripe for a more critical evaluation of the evidence at hand.

It is to be hoped that the scientific community will not allow prejudice to interfere with the submission of new ideas, and will accord the revolutionary views inherent in this work serious and unbiased consideration. Perhaps, by so doing, fresh insight may be obtained which will permit the inquisitive mind of man to draw one small step closer to the elusive goal of Truth.

H.W.G.A.

THE ETERNAL UNIVERSE

THE ETERNAL UNIVERSE

LIST OF ILLUSTRATIONS

THE ETERNAL UNIVERSE

The Universe

Through distant ages man has gazed, with reverence, into the sky;

Foremost in his mind, that momentous question: Why?

How far are yonder points of light,

Shining like tiny beacons on the darkest night?

Whence came the stars, our heavenly host,

Their soft light shimmering like a phantom ghost?

Born of countless suns our Milky Way doth shine,

An enigma to ancient theories, which man must now refine.

Beyond the reaches of our Galaxy, in the enveloping depths of space,

Unnumbered starry systems participate in a truly cosmic race.

For the very universe is expanding, at a most prodigious rate;

Motivated, one would deduce, by Principle: a synonym for Fate.

H.W.G.A.

INTRODUCTION

We find ourselves living in an age which is likely to prove unique in the history of our planet. Never before, during the brief span of a human lifetime, has so much knowledge been made available to an inquisitive mind. It is, in fact, almost as though nature had conspired to finally reveal its most treasured secrets - prior to concluding some great cosmic saga. Whatever the outcome, and regardless of how mankind chooses to utilize this vast influx of scientific insight, the 20th century will probably be looked upon as one of the most crucial epochs of all time. Not only is there the possibility of civilization dooming itself through the folly of nuclear and bacteriological warfare, but the revelations of science may at last suffice to remove much of the mystery which has long frustrated man in his attempts to understand the universe.

Future historians may well refer to our present era as the "Age of Transition." Emerging from the depths of a cloudy evolutionary past, the guiding light of science shines as a promising beacon amidst the darkness of ignorance and superstition. But tradition often dies hard. An inherent reluctance exists to abandon an appealing philosophy or religious viewpoint, no matter how baseless or improbable, unless a more attractive substitute is readily available. Unfortunately, such an alternative has yet to be perfected. This has led to a rather disconcerting spectacle, whereby many aspiring souls are able to glean information sufficient to destroy old concepts - while lacking the capability of formulating a more realistic philosophy in harmony with the new findings of science. The ensuing vacuum cannot avoid leaving many confused and disillusioned with regard to their faith in a meaningful creation. Indeed, as events have turned out, there is presently little correlation of science with the idea of an underlying *Principle or First Cause.* Most assuredly, this is a situation that deserves the utmost consideration.

The real strength of the scientific method lies in the possession of an open mind, and upon a willingness to subject theory to all possible tests. Frequently, at the frontiers of knowledge, circumstantial evidence must be adopted as a basis for establishing the validity of a premise. While this procedure is bound to result in the occasional acceptance of false and misleading interpretations, unlike the case with religious dogmas, there is always the expectation that a scientific falsehood will eventually be uncovered and discarded. It is this very ability to admit past error - regardless of consequences - that characterizes a true scientist, and which has facilitated the enormous progress of recent years.

The immense complexity of the universe has caused science to be divided into multiple fields of inquiry. This specialization is both a blessing and a serious handicap. On the one hand, it is most essential in order to obtain deeper insight into a specific phenomenon. In contrast, it is also a valid point that some phenomena cannot be explained adequately by a single arbitrary branch of science. In truth, a solution may encompass many seemingly diverse fields, *or even have its roots buried in the realm of philosophy!* For this reason one must be extremely careful not to succumb to the "unable to see the forest for the trees" syndrome. In view of the profusion of knowledge that has recently come to light, a most pressing need is to concentrate attention upon the task of molding this information into some comprehensive overall cosmic scheme. Those best qualified to achieve this noble end are likely to be individuals blessed with the attributes of an unbiased philosophical mind, a broad scientific background and, above all, a fervent desire to know the truth.

It is the contention of the author that sufficient clues are now available to link the physical aspect of creation with the *Principle* or *Motivation* upon which it is surely based. To the extent that this work is able to assist one in constructing a more realistic philosophy of life, and to appreciate man's role in a dynamic and evolving cosmos, it shall have accomplished a primary function. To the degree that it succeeds in stimulating a personal search for additional insight, into the many wonders of the universe, it will have fulfilled an even greater purpose.

H.W.G.A.

THE ETERNAL UNIVERSE

Chapter 1

OUR PHYSICAL UNIVERSE

(The Enigma of Matter - Solar Systems - The Stars - Degenerate Stars - The Milky Way - Galaxies of Stars - The Expanding Universe - Quasars.)

Knowledge of the physical structure of our universe is being pursued by science upon two basic fronts - namely, microcosm and macrocosm. On the frontier of microcosm, physicists have succeeded in tapping - for better or for worse - the enormous energy of the atom. On a purely beneficial note, they have also managed to unravel the mystery of the stars, providing valuable insight into the energy processes transpiring deep within their interiors. Astronomers and astrophysicists, concerned with the world of macrocosm, have thus been greatly assisted by research in a branch of science endeavoring to probe in precisely the opposite direction!

Such an instance is typical of the interrelationship which exists among many seemingly diverse fields of inquiry, and affords a graphic illustration of the folly of those who would attempt to exclude philosophical deduction from the realm of science. As long as this approach is capable of explaining phenomena, and is conducive to periodic testing of theory with observation, it provides just as sound a basis as the circumstantial evidence accepted by science in general!

However, before proceeding with this viable principle, which would seek to uncover the Motivation or Purpose behind phenomena, it is necessary to examine certain aspects of our physical universe. Only through an understanding of the laws regulating so-called material structures - ranging from infinitesimal atomic constituents to giant galaxies of stars - is it possible to construct a workable hypothesis that would recognize spiritual motivation as being associated with lowly matter.

THE ETERNAL UNIVERSE

The Enigma of Matter

Throughout the ages matter has commonly been looked upon as an inert and absolutely dead substance, and certainly as having nothing whatever to do with the spiritual aspect of the cosmos from which it was considered to be quite divorced. While, for practical purposes, this contrast in the nature of matter and spirit may have some justification, scientific advances are tending more and more to raise concepts of matter to something above previous rock-bottom estimates - to the status of an enigma, if nothing more. For as strange as it may first seem, the deeper science probes into the secrets of matter the less "materialistic" it actually appears to be!

Take, for example, a tiny molecule of oxygen in the atmosphere we breathe (e.g., two oxygen atoms bound together). Who would dream for one moment that this minute object, measuring only about a hundred millionth of an inch, is constantly darting around and rebounding off other molecules with a velocity of something like a third of a mile per second? Although certain other atoms are not nearly so lively in their habits, they nevertheless are all in a constant state of agitation, ranging from high velocities for gaseous substances down to a more or less rapid vibrating motion for the most rigid solids. Who can honestly consider matter inert and "dead"?

From a dimensional point of view the structure of an atom may be said to consist primarily of empty space! That is to say, its center or nucleus (manifesting positive charges of an influential force known as electricity) is about 10,000 times smaller than the diameter of the atom itself which is extended by a specific number (depending upon the element in question) of much lighter concentrations of mass termed electrons, bearing negative charges of electricity and revolving, so to speak, around the nucleus. Although roughly analogous, in a sense, to that of incredibly minute solar systems, a major difference lies in the realization that electron orbits are constantly shifting so as to envelop the central nucleus in a series of concentric shells.Further evidence has resulted in the firmly established hypothesis of electron spin, in which these tiny particles are seen to resemble rapidly spinning tops - in additionto behaving like miniature magnets by virtue of their negative electric charge.Typically, an atom consists of a central nucleus about 10^{-12} cm in diameter, surrounded by an electron shield occupying a sphere which is roughly 10^{-8} cm in diameter.

The chemical properties of the various elements can be explained on the basis of the number of electrons in the outermost shell. For instance, an atom requiring one more electron to complete its outer shell will readily form a strong bond with another possessing a solitary electron in its most distant shell. (Thus sodium chloride, better known as common salt, is formed when a sodium atom with a "surplus" outer electron is united with a chlorine atom which needs a single electron to complete its outer shell. Two otherwise "aggressive" elements are, in effect, enabled to neutralize each other by reason of their ability to share an outer electron.) In turn, the number of electrons (with negative charge), characterizing a given atom, will depend upon the quantity of protons (with positive charge) in the nucleus, since it is a cardinal rule of nature that unlike electrical charges attract, while like charges repel.

Hydrogen, the simplest element, has a nucleus of but one proton and one encircling electron. Helium, the next heaviest element, has two protons and a completed single shell of two electrons, which accounts for its inert (or neutral) chemical properties. Uranium, at the other end of the scale of natural elements, possesses 92 protons and 92 encircling electrons. The clue as to how numbers of positively charged protons could reside together in a nucleus - without their like charges causing them to fly apart - was provided with the discovery of the neutron by James Chadwick in the year 1932. Still constituting somewhat of a mystery, it is fully evident that they must act as a bonding medium to hold a compound nucleus together. (By way of illustration, a helium nucleus is comprised of two protons and two neutrons - with the neutrons serving to negate the mutual repulsive force of two intimately associated and positively charged protons, while yet permitting them to attract two relatively distant and oppositely charged electrons.)

Essentially stable when bound in atomic nuclei, a free neutron is radioactive and will transform spontaneously into a proton and an electron (plus a small amount of infinitesimal quanta, often referred to as neutrinos) after an average life of about 13 minutes. Electrically neutral, the neutron has a mass equal to roughly 1,839 electrons, being slightly greater than the proton which is rated at about 1,836.5 electron masses. This ability of a free neutron to eject an electron - along with lesser bundles of energy - must surely be of great significance to an understanding of the basic structure of matter. Indeed, it provides ample proof that material particles are composed of varying amounts of "congealed energy" that has simply become fused together. Most assuredly, matter is of a decidedly divisible nature!

Instead of our being able to resolve matter into a few inert and unchangeable substances, as was once supposed, we now find our so-called physical universe to be built out of what might best be described as divisible and interchangeable condensations of energy or forces - of "fields of influence" of varying strength. Clearly, it is a medium which defies explanation upon a purely mechanical basis, and which exhibits properties quite in contrast to the "dead" substance that our imperfect senses would lead us to picture. It has been said that electricity is a basic commodity out of which our universe is constructed. But just what is electricity? Moreover, what is the equally mysterious force of gravitation? Perhaps the conspicuous failure of modern science to resolve such enigmas is an indication that an entirely new approach is in order - presumably, one in which the idea of Principle or spiritual Motivation is assigned a prominent role! After all, at the level of biological life, does not mere physical matter succeed in manifesting what might be termed spirit or soul? Has science been guilty, in effect, of inadvertently drawing a line between matter and spirit - when, in truth, no line can be drawn?

To summarize, it may be stated that the two fundamental particles of matter, which alone possess the ability to exist in a free and stable state, are the proton and electron - or their oppositely charged counterparts, the anti-proton and positron. Extremely rare, in our region of the universe, these counterparts have only a transient existence, being annihilated in collisions with common matter. Positrons, for example, will readily unite with far more numerous free electrons to produce binary pairs of high energy gamma rays. For some very good reason, which must be ascribed to circumstances surrounding the initial creation of matter itself, virtually no anti-protons were allowed to survive. Likewise, relatively very few free positrons have been permitted to inhabit our region of space. This is just as well, of course, since the presence of large numbers of these oppositely charged entities would lead to a chaotic annihilation of material particles and a universe consisting of little else than pure energy! Invariably, this biased production and distribution of fundamental particles must be given due consideration by any theory attempting to account for the origin of our physical universe.

Solar Systems

As we all know, the Sun occupies the central position in our Solar System. Essentially a huge ball of intensely hot gas, it has a surface temperature of almost 6,000°C. and an internal temperature of something like 13,000,000°C. at its center. The Earth's own diameter of almost 8,000 miles appears rather paltry in comparison to that of the Sun's stupendous 864,000 miles. In mass or weight it is roughly a third of a million times greater than the Earth, containing (by weight) about 75% hydrogen, 20% helium, and approximately 5% of all the remaining heavier elements. The density of the Sun varies considerably at different depths, in the sense that the central regions are exceedingly dense while the outer layers are comprised of gases existing in a somewhat rarefied state. Although the Sun is some 93 million miles distant from us, it is not its particularly high luminosity but rather its comparative nearness which is responsible for its appearing so much more brilliant than the stars. Indeed, as great a contrast as there may seem to be, our Sun is simply an average star! It just happens to be the closest.

Of all the planets in our Solar System, only the Earth is suitable for the evolution of higher life forms. Mercury, the closest body to the Sun at a scant 36 million miles, is practically a facsimile of our barren and airless Moon. Venus, almost the size of the Earth and the next planet in order from the Sun at a distance of some 67 million miles, is characterized by extremely high surface temperatures and a dense carbon dioxide atmosphere many times greater than our own. Mars, the last of the inner planets at some 1½ times the Earth's distance from the Sun, is about 4,200 miles in diameter and lacks sufficient gravity to retain much of an atmosphere. Resembling Jupiter's larger moons, in certain respects, Mars offers little hope of life having ever developed much beyond a microscopic stage. Jupiter and Saturn, the gas giants of our system with masses some 317 and 95 times that of Earth, orbit the Sun at distances of 482 million miles and 888 million miles, respectively. Uranus, almost 15 times as heavy as the Earth, is a little over 19 times more distant. Neptune, the last of the semi-giants of our planetary family at a distance of nearly 2.8 billion miles, weighs slightly more than 17 times that of our Earth. At the very fringe of the Solar System lies the planet Pluto, pursuing an eccentric orbit which carries it as far as 4.6 billion miles from the Sun. Now known to be smaller than the Moon, it must have a surface temperature that is perpetually hundreds of degrees below zero.

There are two other phenomena, belong to our Solar System, which deserve special mention on the grounds that they contain clues as to its origin. Lying chiefly between the orbits of Mars and Jupiter are swarms of smaller bodies known as asteroids. They range in size from giant Ceres, some 480 miles in diameter, to the dimensions of mere boulders and pebbles. Such bodies represent a combination of primordial material which simply failed to form another planet, and evolving bodies that collided and disintegrated during the early history of our Solar System. The second phenomenon is that of comets, many billions of which are believed to encircle the Sun as a distant halo some tens of billions of miles out in space. Comprised mainly of frozen gases, interspersed with varying amounts of dust and other solid bodies, they constitute remnants of the epic process of planetary formation that took place shortly after the Sun's birth some 5 billion years ago.

Since one of the original discoveries about our Solar System involved the knowledge that all of the planets revolve in the same direction as the Sun rotates, and on virtually the same plane as the Sun's equator, it was inevitable that this remarkable coincidence should inspire ideas as to the origin of our family of planets. Accordingly, it was not long before theory was advanced to the effect that the Sun and planets were formed, at about the same time, from the condensation of a huge cloud of interstellar gas and dust. In conformity to a firmly established principle of physics, whereby contraction of a rotating body must lead to an increase in its rate of spin, it was assumed that when our protosun had shrunk to a critical degree strong rotary forces must have caused periodic ejections of material - from whence the planets and their moons later condensed. Yet another line of reasoning tended to support this common origin hypothesis. Gravitation, for instance, would tend to contract such a gas cloud into one huge mass - not multitudes of smaller bodies comprising the planets, satellites, asteroids and comets.

Unfortunately, as is sometimes the way in science, the obvious solution begins to run into trouble when additional (but only partial) information becomes available. In this case it was eventually shown that the Sun, containing more than 99% of all the matter in our Solar System, actually possesses only about 2% of the total angular momentum - the property that keeps the Sun rotating and the planets revolving around it. How was it possible, critics wanted to know, for planets having less than 1% of a system's mass to acquire a staggering 98% of its angular momentum? In effect, to balance the mathematics of the system it would be necessary to either increase the Sun's rotation by an enormous factor, or else have the planets orbiting at a very small fraction of their present distance! So impressive is this objection that, for some decades, it was deemed sufficient to completely rule out the idea that planets could have formed from a rapidly rotating protosun. Consequently, a variety of alternate theories were seriously entertained for over half a century, all of which relegated the formation of planetary systems to the status of a rare cosmic fluke.

But it was to prove a classic example of a little knowledge serving only to obscure an issue. The clue to a solution of this problem was eventually uncovered through a study of stellar rotations, when it became evident that some external force must have acted to drastically slow the Sun's rate of spin. Considering the vast distances over which primordial gas clouds must contract, it would take very little original motion in order to achieve rotary forces capable of bringing about the inferred separation of material long before contraction reached stellar diameters. From a study of recently formed stars it became clear that rotation speeds of a hundred times or more were the rule rather than the exception! (Pleione, an extremely hot young star of the Pleiades cluster, may be cited as an example of a star rotating with such rapidity that it has developed a conspicuous flattened disk at its equator.) Since this persistent increase of rotation - with respect to both age and mass - is far beyond what can be accounted for by a minor increase in the initial diameter of an interstellar gas cloud condensing into a star of slightly greater mass, it becomes rather obvious that some external force must be involved in the relatively late stages of stellar formation.

THE ETERNAL UNIVERSE

Assuming that the rotational velocity of a newborn star has thus increased to the point where a ring of gas has been expelled from the equator, there remains a crucial twofold problem. First, it is necessary to explain how the rotation of our Sun was reduced from mere hours to almost a month. Secondly, by what means was the gaseous disk pushed to the relatively enormous distances of the planetary orbits? As events were to turn out, a solution to the one problem was also to afford an answer for the other. While radiation pressure was seen to play a definite role in driving outward large amounts of uncondensed hydrogen and helium, recognition of the existence and properties of an intense magnetic field was to supply the missing key ingredient.

The modest magnetic field of a typical gas cloud will be enhanced dramatically upon contraction to stellar dimensions. With the presence of just such a strong magnetic field, between the newly formed Sun and its rapidly rotating ring of gaseous material, it becomes possible to infer a solution to both problems. For the very act of transferring rotational momentum to the gaseous ring, thereby causing it to be pushed further and further away, would also serve as the external force required to act as a brake upon the Sun's rotation. With the passage of time, the material of the disk would be repelled to considerable distances, where it could condense into the planets and satellites, while the Sun's rotation became slowed to the value we now observe. As might be anticipated, one important consequence of this process must be a gradual reduction of the Sun's magnetic field to its present strength.

Since the initial chemical composition of the rotating ring must have been the same as that of our Sun, it is clear that a high percentage of such lighter elements as hydrogen and helium must have been dispersed altogether from our Solar System. On the other hand, it is logical to suspect that the heavier elements will be the least affected and will accumulate in orbits closest to the Sun. Observation does, in fact, substantiate this premise, revealing that the four inner planets (Mercury, Venus, Earth and Mars) do possess an abundance of heavier elements over the outer planets, and in essentially this order. The end of this belt of heavier elements seems to have been reached between the orbits of Mars and Jupiter, where swarms of small rock and nickel-iron asteroids are found. Along with the intense impact cratering of planets and satellites alike, such debris testifies as mute evidence of the accretion process which transpired during earlier stages of our system's history. The huge planets of our solar family, Jupiter and Saturn, had evidently accumulated sufficient mass to trap appreciable quantities of the lighter elements before they had passed beyond their orbits. Hence hydrogen, by far the most abundant element, became a chief constituent of these planets. It would appear that the planets lying beyond the orbit of Saturn were somewhat later in condensing, and so managed to acquire smaller amounts of hydrogen and are accordingly less massive.

Inasmuch as our Sun is an average star, it must follow that vast numbers of other planetary systems are bound to have arisen in a similar way. Even allowing for the likelihood that many of these potentialities will be wasted, for one reason or another, it is impossible to escape the conviction that at least a substantial proportion of them will result in the formation of planets comparable to our Earth. The total number of probable abodes of biological life must surely be in the billions within the confines of our own Milky Way galaxy alone, and billions of billions within the expanse of the entire universe! As to the question of whether life similar to our own will develop on these other worlds, we have only to ponder the notions of certain misguided ancestors who once thought in terms of a flat Earth situated at the center of the universe. Clearly, this inescapable conclusion must dominate all future philosophical inquiry into the nature of the cosmos!

The Stars

Moving away from the limiting dimensions of our Solar System, we now turn to the fascinating subject of the stars themselves. The method used in determining the distances of the nearer stars is really quite simple in principle, although in actual practice the measurements involved entail a high degree of accuracy. As a result of the Earth's revolution around the Sun, certain stars will sppear to describe a slight backwards and forwards motion with respect to the more distant stars in the background. By means of mathematical calculation, utilizing this annual displacement (or "parallax"), it can be readily shown that even the closest star is exceedingly remote - some 25 million million miles away! In order to express such great distances more conveniently, the term "light year" has been adopted. A light year is the distance covered in one year by a ray of light traveling at the speed of

186,000 miles per second, or almost 6 million million miles. In this manner the nearest star has been found to be some 4.3 light years away while Sirius, the brightest star in the sky, is at a distance of about 8.6 light years.

While the Sun itself is several light years distant from the nearest star, a large proportion of the stars are much closer to one another. In fact, many of them (perhaps more than half) are so close that their spacing is more nearly planetary than stellar. Such pairs of stars revolving about a common center form what are known as binary systems, and have been found with periods as long as many thousands of years for the more distant members down to a matter of hours for some stars that are almost in actual contact. Binary systems are of great value to the astronomer, since by observing the orbits of these stars it is possible to calculate their masses with a surprising degree of success.

Once the distances of stars have been measured, it then becomes feasible to determine their true brightness (e.g., absolute magnitude). When this has been done such comparatively distant stars as Canopus, Rigel, Deneb and Betelgeuse are actually found to be many thousands of times more luminous than our Sun; while on the other hand many of the nearer stars are much fainter (e.g., Proxima Centauri, at a distance of little more than 4 light years, is only 1/10,000th as bright as the Sun). Thus it will be seen that the apparent or visual brightness of a star is no positive guide as to its true distance, since the stars themselves differ enormously in luminosity.

Although most stars may first appear alike in color to the naked eye, closer investigation reveals that there is really an appreciable difference between them. Some stars like Rigel and Sirius shine with a bluish and whitish glow, while others like Arcturus and Antares are orange and red respectively; the Sun itself is a yellow star. These differences of color range from purple and blue downwards through white, yellow, orange, bright red, to finally a dull red, and serve as an excellent indication as to a star's surface temperature - the purple and blue stars being quite hot, about 12,000°C. upwards, while the red stars are much cooler with temperatures of 3,000°C. or less. As the true brightness of an object depends upon both the temperature and the total surface area it is easy to show that the difference in temperature alone is insufficient to account for the wide range in the absolute magnitudes of the various stars. It must surely follow that some stars possess far greater radiating surfaces than others!

Observation reveals that this is indeed the case. In fact, the range in the sizes of the stars is exceedingly large. While most stars do not differ too greatly in diameter from our Sun and belong to what is known as the "main-sequence" (e.g., stars that have experienced little evolutionary change), there are some so large that if one of them were to replace the Sun the orbits of the inner planets would actually lie within the body of the star itself! Although in general these huge stars have relatively low surface temperatures their enormous sizes are sufficient to make them objects of exceptionally high luminosity. Such stars may exceed the Sun's diameter by literally hundreds of times, and are known as red giants and supergiants. At the other extreme are stars so small that while they possess the mass of stars they resemble the planet Earth in size. Objects failing into this category are referred to as white dwarfs, and are generally quite hot, usually white or blue. As if this is not enough, even more compacted structures have been found to exist in the form of neutron stars, typically about 20 miles in diameter and twice the mass of the Sun!

Despite the wide range in the sizes of the stars their masses exhibit surprisingly little variation, with the vast majority having masses between one-fifth and five times that of the Sun. It is therefore follows that the stars must display a most remarkable variety of densities. For example, when the enormous volumes of the red giants are compared with their masses, the average density is found to be less than a millionth that of the Sun, or much less than the density of our own atmosphere! They are truly inflated stars in every sense of the word. In the other direction, the much smaller white dwarfs are so dense that a cubic inch of their material must weigh many tons. Even more bizarre is the compressed state of matter characterizing neutron stars, where a single tablespoonful of material would weigh an estimated 40 billion tons!

By comparing the luminosities of the various stars with their masses, it was discovered that of the stars belonging to the main-sequence the blue stars are somewhat larger and heavier than the Sun; while the red ones are all smaller and less massive. In other words, the surface temperatures of main-sequence stars are determined essentially by their masses, in the sense that the heavier stars are the hottest and therefore are radiating larger quantities of energy into surrounding space. However, it is important to note that the amount of energy so radiated increases at a much more rapid rate than can be accounted for by a simple increase in the mass of a star. This point is of particular significance inasmuch as it means that the more massive stars will exhaust their supplies of fuel in a comparatively short time, and so meet their ultimate fate in but a fraction of the lifetime of the average star!

While the overwhelming majority of stars remain of constant temperature and brightness like our Sun, there are certain exceptions which display very noticeable fluctuations of a periodic nature. Discounting those instances where the variations are caused by the mutual eclipses of two revolving stars (eclipsing variables), the remainder may be attributed to a rhythmic contraction and expansion of the star itself. Triggered by internal instability such a star becomes heated with each contraction and expands until its gaseous atmosphere has cooled sufficiently to allow gravitation to prevail, and so induce yet another contraction. The group of variables having periods measured in hours are usually referred to as RR Lyrae stars; while those with cycles ranging from about 2 to 40 days are classed as Cepheid variables.

What became so highly significant about these regular fluctuations was the fact that there is a strong relationship between the intrinsic brightness of the star and its period of pulsation. In brief, it was discovered that the stars with the longer periods were also objects of far greater brilliance than the ones with shorter cycles. With knowledge of the true brightness of similar pulsating stars within the range of parallax, or other comparatively short distance techniques, it was at once possible to determine the real luminosity of any star for which a characteristic pulsation period was evident. In this way it was found that a Cepheid with a cycle of 2 days was about 1,000 times as bright as the Sun, while one with a period of little more than a month was some 20,000 times as luminous. (Polaris, the North Pole Star, is a typical Cepheid with a pulsation cycle of about 4 days.) As it is impossible to measure the parallax of a star with any degree of accuracy beyond a distance of a few hundred light years, and since Cepheid variables are objects of very high luminosity, it will be seen that this particular group of stars has been of invaluable assistance in mapping the more distant reaches of the Milky Way, and even to neighboring exterior systems.

THE ETERNAL UNIVERSE

Degenerate Stars

To grasp the peculiar sequence of events which link bloated red giants with the crushed state of the white dwarfs, it is necessary to understand what determines the size of a star of given mass. The diameter of a star is actually the outcome of two opposing forces. On the one hand, we have the force of gravitation which tends to draw all matter into a common center of infinite density. Opposed to this unifying influence is the explosive or repulsive force of heat - in essence, motion which acts to drive the material of a star apart. Condensing out of a hydrogen-rich gas cloud a newly formed star will cease contracting when sufficient heat is generated, deep within its central core, to support the weight of all overlying layers. At this point it will stop shrinking and become a normal main-sequence star like our Sun, with its surface temperature being a distinct reflection of mass - in the sense that large purple-blue colored stars are the heaviest and hottest, and dull red stars the coolest and smallest.

Initially, this heat comes from the tremendous compression produced through gravitational contraction. When the central regions of a star reach a critical temperature nuclear reactions are started which convert hydrogen into helium with the release of a substantial and steady flow of energy. The amount of energy generated in this manner is determined by such factors as chemical composition and mass. Of the two, mass plays a truly fundamental role. The reason for this may be attributed to the fact that increased mass leads to higher internal temperature and, subsequently, to an acceleration in the rate of nuclear reactions which are greatly facilitated by even a modest rise of temperature. This increase in a star's radiation output is out of all proportion to a simple addition of mass. Thus the ultraviolet giant Rigel, 30 times heavier than the Sun, shines with a brilliance 40,000 times as great! As a direct consequence of this state of affairs the lifetime of a star is very much regulated by the amount of material it contains. Instead of the more massive stars having more fuel to burn over a longer period of time, it is quite the reverse. Stars of greater mass will expend their supplies of energy in a comparatively short interval, and so meet their ultimate fate in but a fraction of the time needed by the slower burning lightweight stars to exhaust their fuel.

THE ETERNAL UNIVERSE

By the middle of the 20th century it became a generally accepted truth that a star will commence expanding as it consumes its supply of hydrogen, very slowly at first and then at a steadily increasing pace as changes in chemical composition and distribution begin to have their effect. As the outer atmosphere of an evolving star expands and becomes cooler and less dense, exactly the opposite conditions prevail deep in the interior. A central core of helium ash is formed and continues to grow in size as more and more hydrogen is converted to this end product. Gravitational contraction of this core leads to higher temperatures which, in turn, allows hydrogen-burning reactions to occur with greater efficiency and over a larger volume of the star's interior. As this energy-producing region begins to move outward from the center the outer layers of the star are literally blasted further and further apart, and the star is induced to move off the main-sequence enroute to the realm of the inflated red giants. Although it has taken our Sun roughly five billion years to evolve to its present state, which is only slightly removed from its original status, one more such interval will lead to profound changes. Red dwarf stars of smaller mass have normal life expectancies measured in tens of billions of years. At the other extreme are certain heavyweights whose spendthrift nature will cause them to evolve significantly in less than a hundred million years.

What happens after a critical proportion of a star's hydrogen is consumed? Upon reaching the stage where the generation of nuclear energy is insufficient to support a star's outer regions, the expansion process is reversed and a degree of gravitational collapse is initiated. As a result of this contraction the star will temporarily become heated and undergo expansion (perhaps ejecting a small portion of its atmosphere) until subsequent cooling permits another contraction. In effect, it may now be transformed into a pulsating star, of which the Cepheids are typical examples of one particular class or stage of evolution. As such a star continues to shrink, under the influence of gravitation, its dull red surface changes as it passes through successively hotter colors. Contracting far beyond its initial status on the main-sequence it may eventually become a small but rather hot dwarf star - essentially, a white dwarf of high density.

Not all stars are privileged to follow this evolutionary loop without interruption, or to end their lives as white dwarfs. Extreme violence seems to lie in store for exceptionally massive stars.

THE ETERNAL UNIVERSE

Long before a heavy star is able to consume all of its hydrogen the helium core will reach temperatures conducive to the formation of more complex elements. Helium is converted into such elements as carbon, oxygen, neon, etc., with subsequent contraction of the core leading to ever higher temperatures. In due course heavier and heavier elements are built up in layers within the star, with the ultimate iron group of heavy metals at the center arising from the burning of the silicon group which had preceded it. With the build-up of an incredibly dense iron-rich core of atomic nuclei, floating in a virtual sea of electrons, the stage is rapidly being set for a momentous event. Once this core reaches a critical mass and temperature, electrons are squeezed inside the heavy nuclei where they unite with oppositely charged protons to form neutrons. Occupying less space than that of their combined separate identities, the collapse of the core is accelerated - resulting in ever greater numbers of neutrons being formed and an even faster rate of contraction. This eventually leads to a runaway collapse and a catastrophic implosion of the core. The enormous energy suddenly released by this event is sufficient to detonate all of the remaining unburned elements in the rest of the doomed star - producing a monstrous explosion known as a supernova, in which radiation is released equal to the light of hundreds of millions of suns! Having thus rid itself of much of its mass the stellar remnant is allowed to pursue evolution to its predestined status of a neutron star, or beyond.

Dramatic as a supernova may be it is not an isolated phenomenon without cosmic purpose. Were it not for these stupendous explosions, which effectively shatter the more massive stars, biological life would have been quite impossible. This is due to the fact that virtually all elements heavier than hydrogen (with the probable exception of limited amounts of helium) are produced exclusively in the interiors of stars, especially heavy stars destined as supernovae candidates. It is only through explosions of extreme violence that these vital ingredients manage to become interspersed with clouds of otherwise almost pure hydrogen gas, so that later generations of stars are able to condense out of just the required medium to give birth to planets with the proper chemical composition. Of the matter comprising our very bodies, most of it was invariably once part of a supernova!

THE ETERNAL UNIVERSE

The eventual fate of a degenerate star hinges upon the crucial issue of mass, which allows but three choices: namely, white dwarf, neutron star, or black hole. Stability is reached, in the case of white dwarf stars, by means of what is termed degenerate electron pressure. In effect, atomic nuclei are able to float contentedly in a sea of tightly packed electrons - as long as the star's gravitational field does not exceed a critical value! By calculation, this figure is equivalent to some 1.4 solar masses, and is known as the Chandrasekhar limit. Degenerate stars heavier than this value cannot resist the intense force of gravitation, which will serve to crush matter to still greater densities. Confirmation of this interpretation is provided by observation, since no white dwarf star has been found with a mass in excess of this crucial 1.4 solar mass limit.

The next stage of compression beyond white dwarfdom is that of a neutron star, which is formed when the electron sea is forced inside proton nuclei - producing what is tantamount to a super atomic particle comprised of neutrons. But just as white dwarf stars have their restrictions with regard to mass, so do neutron stars. In fact, it turns out to be a rather narrow limit, with the subsequent degenerate neutron pressure stage incapable of restraining gravity much beyond about 2.5 solar masses. Although white dwarf stars are exceedingly plentiful and have been observed for some time, neutron stars are much less common and it was not until 1967 that the first one was finally identified on a photographic plate. Even then, it was as a result of attention being focused upon the origin of strange radio signals from space. A star at the center of the Crab Nebula (an acknowledged supernova remnant that became visible in the year 1054 A.D.) was found to be flashing on and off some 30 times per second, in perfect synchronization with the radio pulses. Generally referred to as pulsars, such objects are believed to be fast spinning neutron stars embedded in incredibly powerful magnetic fields. Characterized by pulsation periods commensurate with their rotation, they have been described in terms of whirling celestial lighthouse beacons.

The ultimate state of compression is the inevitable fate awaiting degenerate stars possessing masses in excess of what can be supported by this last resort of degenerate neutron pressure. As bizarre as it may seem, the relentless force of gravitation will cause contraction to proceed with ever increasing efficiency - literally squashing the star out of being! Without a doubt, an implosion of space and time must ensue, producing a situation in which even radiation is unable to escape against the overwhelming force of gravity. A singularity of this order is a stellar black hole, and may be detected only by its influence on surrounding matter. (The strong X-ray source known as Cygnus X-1, in the immediate vicinity of a star cataloged as HDE226868, was the first of a number of stellar black hole candidates to be discovered. Its presence is believed to be revealed through radiation emitted from gases, ejected previously by its binary companion to form an accretion disk about the black hole, and now in the process of being accelerated to enormous velocities as it spirals toward the rapidly whirling infinitesimal core of the singularity.) Essentially, a black hole may be described as an entity that has severed connections with the empirical universe and has entered a new and entirely different realm of cosmic existence!

The Milky Way

Just as planets are members of aggregations known as solar systems, so the Sun and many billions of other stars are combined to form a vastly greater structure: our Galaxy, also referred to as the Milky Way. In general shape our Galaxy bears some resemblance to a fried egg, in that its central nucleus is much thicker and more dense than the outlying regions which tend to trail away at the edges. Through a study of 21-cm radiation, radio telescopes have succeeded in mapping the far reaches of our Milky Way, revealing a basic spiral structure that is so common among the exterior systems. Containing by weight about 1.4×10^{11} (140 billion) solar masses, our Galaxy is probably comprised of something like 400 billion individual stars, extending over a region of the order of 100,000 light years. With a thickness about 1/10th of its diameter, the lense-shaped main body of our system is enveloped by a spherical halo of more sparsely distributed stars. In every sense of the word, it is truly an enormous concentration of suns.

Like the discovery that our Earth is not at the center of the universe, so astronomers have determined that the Sun is not located within the central bulge of our Galaxy, but is instead situated between two spiral arms roughly 30,000 light years from the galactic nucleus. With an orbital motion of close to 150 miles per second, it takes our Sun almost 250 million years to complete one full circuit around the center of our Galaxy. The broad band of encircling light, which may best be observed stretching across the sky on a clear moonless night, is called the Milky Way and owes its appearance to our location near the central plane of our highly flattened system.

In some sections of the Milky Way the stars are so numerous that their light has blended into what appear to be huge cumulus clouds - clouds which cannot be resolved into separate stars except with the aid of a good telescope. In addition to these mammoth star fields, our Galaxy is especially rich in many smaller yet more compact accumulations of stars known as open or galactic clusters, of which the Pleides and Hyades clusters are among those in which the brighter members are visible to the naked eye. As a casual glance will show, the Milky Way is not one continuous stream of light but contains many conspicuous regions which seem almost devoid of stars. These dark sections, of which the "Great Rift" in the Northern Hemisphere and the "Coalsack" near the Southern Cross are the most famous, are not actually caused by a lack of stars in these regions but are due to obscuring clouds of fine dust lying between us and the otherwise brilliant star fields of the Milky Way. These huge clouds of dust serve to scatter and dim the light from the more distant stars, thus effectively preventing us from viewing what lies beyond. In this manner the central nucleus of our Galaxy is forever hidden to optical observation behind vast clouds of interstellar dust. Such dark areas are the product of ancient supernovae explosions, in which large amounts of gas and dust are ejected violently into space, where they must eventually mix with uncondensed hydrogen to form an enriched mixture of various elements and molecular compounds - exactly the composition required for later generations of stars to give birth to habitable planets!

This enrichment of interstellar gas clouds, through the process of supernovae explosions, has resulted in the existence of two basic types of stellar population: namely, metal-poor and metal-rich stars. The former constitute the oldest stars in our Galaxy (having been born in a primeval environment consisting of almost pure hydrogen with, perhaps, a little helium), and are believed to have ages of at least 15 billion years. The second group of stars are all younger members of our Milky Way, and are characterized by a much higher proportion of nature's heavier elements. Situated near the galactic plane, our Sun is a metal-rich star due to its somewhat later birth in a gaseous nebula enriched from earlier generations of supernovae. In contrast, the spherical halo of stars is populated by a preponderance of older metal-poor inhabitants, by reason of a lack of uncondensed nebulae so essential for the formation of new stars.

Although optical telescopes are unable to penetrate the opaque dust clouds which hide the nucleus of our Galaxy, this is fortunately not the case with regard to radio observation. The picture to emerge is one of considerable interest. Instead of a simple concentration of more closely packed stars, with faster rotation periods, there is evidence that other energetic events are taking place. The center of our Galaxy, in the constellation of Sagittarius, is the origin of a number of noteworthy phenomena. An expanding ring of hydrogen gas, equivalent to at least several million solar masses, is streaming outward as though expelled from a gigantic explosion about 10 million years ago. In addition, a strong source of microwaves is emanating from an encircling ring of dust and gas roughly 2,000 light years in diameter. This cloud is also expanding outward, with a velocity of close to 25 miles per second in this instance. Still closer to the center is an extremely powerful radio source known as Sagittarius A. Coming from a region only about 40 light years in diameter, it is a strong emitter of synchrotron radiation - being produced by high-speed electrons spiraling around an intense magnetic field. The only conceivable explanation involves the presence of a supermassive rotating black hole at the center of our Galaxy, possibly of the order of 5 million solar masses if a recent study of fast moving gases near the galactic core is any indication. This interpretation is given further support by the discovery of strong gamma ray radiation stemming from this very same region. Uncovered by means of a satellite borne gamma ray detector, this is precisely what might be inferred from the generating properties of a powerful rotating black hole dynamo!

Forming a concentric halo about the nucleus of our Galaxy, like a swarm of orbiting satellites at distances measured in tens of thousands of light years, are several hundred globular clusters. Typically a hundred light years or so in diameter, and containing upwards of 100,000 suns, they are exceedingly compact aggregations of older, metal-poor, first generation stars. Featuring relatively large numbers of pulsating RR Lyrae variables, and almost no uncondensed gas and dust clouds with which to form new stars, their common origin and distance made it easy for astronomers to notice the correlation of intrinsic luminosity with pulsation period. Their pronounced distribution about the galactic nucleus also served to give man the first indication of his eccentric location in the Milky Way.

Situated in the Southern Hemisphere, and appearing as two fuzzy patches of light on a clear moonless night, are twin satellite systems known as the Magellanic Clouds. Classified as small irregular galaxies, both are comprised of many millions of stars and possess a mixed population with regard to age and chemical composition. The Large Magellanic Cloud is about 160,000 light years distant; while the Small Magellanic Cloud is slightly further away at a distance of some 190,000 light years. Like the swarms of smaller globular clusters, they give the impression of being remnants left over from the formation of our Milky Way.

Galaxies of Stars

Galaxies come in a wide assortment of sizes and shapes. Often described in terms of four basic classifications (e.g., elliptical, spiral, barred spiral and irregular), further subdivision is capable of imparting additional information. Thus a spiral galaxy with tightly wound arms and a rather fat central bulge is called an Sa system; one with a moderately large central nucleus and moderately wound arms is defined as an Sb galaxy; while loosely wound arms extending from a relatively small nucleus is characteristic of a type Sc system. (our own Milky Way falls into the category of an Sb galaxy.) Due chiefly to the fact that there are large numbers of small and dwarf ellipticals, the overall distribution of exterior systems is believed to consist of roughly 60% elliptical, 20% spiral, 10% barred spiral and 10% irregular.

In the constellation of Andromeda, at a distance of a little over 2 million light years, lies the beautiful spiral galaxy known as M31. This great star system is, in many respects, a twin to our own Galaxy. Similar in both size and shape to the Milky Way, it is even encircled by a comparable retinue of globular clusters and possesses a like number of Cepheid variables in its spiral arms. Along with about a dozen and a half smaller systems, mostly of the dwarf elliptical type, these two large galaxies comprise what is known as the Local Group - a weak gravitationally bound cluster some 2.5 million light years or so in diameter.

Moving outward to a distance of almost 7 million light years, we come to another small cluster which is dominated by the spiral galaxy M81. Located in the constellation of Ursa Major, this system could also qualify as a twin to our Galaxy. Other prominent members include NGC2403, a small spiral system, and the irregular galaxy M82. Many similar small groupings are to be found as still greater distances are probed. For instance, in the constellation of Canes Venatici, the much photographed "Whirlpool Galaxy" is observed as a major component of yet another weakly bound gravitational association. Also known as M51, this galaxy is associated with such spiral systems as M101, M63, M94 and NGC4258, all of which are about 14 million light years distant.

A very noticeable departure takes place, some 60 million light years away, in the direction of the constellation Virgo. Instead of sparse aggregations of galaxies, only a few of which may be considered to contain really large star systems, an extremely rich cluster is finally encountered. Centered by the supergiant elliptical (almost spherical) galaxy called M87, the sprawling Virgo Cloud contains many substantial members and is the closest example of some of the dense swarms which exist. (A monster among galaxies, M87 is no ordinary concentration of stars. Not only is it an exceptionally massive system, emitting prodigious amounts of radio waves and X-rays, but its turbulent central core is believed to contain an enormous black hole of the order of some 5 billion solar masses!) The giant Virgo Cloud forms the nucleus of a vast assemblage of lesser clusters and associated groupings - including our own Local Group - which has come to be known as the Local Supercluster. Similarly, as the Sun is not centrally located, so our Milky Way is revealed to be situated at the outskirts of this overall aggregation.

Typically, a supercluster contains several thousand members and tends to be spread out over a zone about 150 million light years or more across. With an average separation between supercluster centers focusing upon a figure of roughly half a billion or so light years, immense voids are now seen to be interspersed with such galactic clumpings. Extending, upon occasion, to distances at least 300 million light years in diameter, one of these seemingly empty voids could actually accommodate many

THE ETERNAL UNIVERSE

thousands of Milky Way galaxies. A subject of growing interest among astronomers, superclusters appear to be distributed in a remarkably uniform manner when viewed upon the large-scale, and evidently constitute the ultimate degree of structuring within the universe.

The Expanding Universe

The principle of the Doppler effect, first expounded by the 19th century physicist Christian Doppler, is crucial to an understanding of what must be considered a truly fundamental feature of the universe. Just as with sound waves, radiation from an approaching source will result in a bunching up of signals and a shift to shorter wavelengths. Conversely, a receding source will cause radiation to be spread out more thinly and shifted to longer wavelengths. Moreover, for many practical purposes, the degree of this displacement is essentially in proportion to the speed of relative motion - in the sense that the greater the velocity, the greater the wavelength shift. Since the light of a luminous astronomical object may be readily broken down to various reference points, by means of passing it through the prism of a spectroscopic device, it became feasible to determine speeds of approach or recession simply by measuring the amount of such displacement from normal or "rest wavelengths." In this manner scientists were able to show that a shift in wavelength, toward the blue end of the spectrum, was indicative of a certain speed of approach; while a shift in the opposite direction, toward the longer wavelength of red light, was a clear indication of a specific motion of recession.

The procedure soon became a powerful tool with which to deduce a wide variety of celestial facts, ranging from the revolutions of stellar binary systems to the rotations and movements of entire galaxies of stars. Utilizing this spectroscopic technique the astronomer Vesto Slipher, of Lowell Observatory, came up with a rather amazing discovery by the year 1925. Inexplicably, some 38 out of the 40 spiral nebulae that he had investigated showed unmistakable evidence of recession! Furthermore, he had measured speeds as great as 2% of the velocity of light itself - an incredibly high degree of motion in those days.

THE ETERNAL UNIVERSE

The full significance of this peculiarity was not appreciated until 1929, when another astronomer by the name of Edwin Hubble supplied the missing clue. Having recently proven that the heretofore mysterious "spiral nebulae" were really distant galaxies of stars, it was noticed that a most remarkable relationship existed when the velocities of receding galaxies were compared with their distances. Without a doubt, the more remote systems were receding at greater speeds than nearby galaxies. In effect, once distances beyond our Local Group were examined, the entire universe was observed to be in a state of expansion! That is to say, except for relatively small gravitationally bound clusters, the galaxies were all receding from each other - and with speeds evidently in direct proportion to distance! Thus a cluster situated at twice the distance of another was found to be rushing away at twice the velocity. Likewise, one at triple the distance was seen to be receding at triple the speed, etc. Known as Hubble's constant, this rate of expansion of the universe may be defined as a measure of the time required for a receding system to double its velocity of recession. In terms of philosophical implication, it was to be one of the most important revelations of the century!

Applying this remarkable distance-velocity proportionality relationship (generally referred to as the Hubble law) to galaxies so remote as to preclude distance determination by other reliable means, it has been possible to map the brighter cluster members out to distances involving billions of light years. Accordingly, a supercluster in the constellation of Ursa Major, with a redshift of some 9,300 miles per second, is receding at about 5% of the velocity of light and is believed to be at least 900 million light years away. Another supercluster in Corona Borealis is redshifted to the equivalent of 13,400 miles per second, which is indicative of a recession velocity 7.2% that of light and a distance of roughly 1.3 billion light years (BLY). In the constellation of Bootes, a supercluster has been found with a redshift implying a recession of 24,400 miles per second, translating to about 13% that of light and a distance of 2.3 BLY. Yet another supercluster, in the constellation of Hydra, is redshifted to the extent of 38,000 miles per second, which is equal to a speed 20.4% that of light and a distance of some 3.68 BLY. Upon this basis the "observable universe" has been acknowledged by astronomers to have a radius of about 18 BLY, which corresponds to redshift increments of a little more than 10 miles per second per million light years of separation. At such a distance any velocity of recession is assumed to be equal to the speed of light and, by tradition, would preclude all possibility of viewing what (if anything) lies beyond.

For some decades astrophysicists have been inclined to denote the degree of redshift by the letter "Z". Essentially, for low velocities, Z is equal to the amount of spectral displacement expressed as a similar fraction of the speed of light. An object redshifted by 5% would be said to possess a redshift of $Z = .05$; while one displaced 10% would be rated as $Z = .10$, etc. This simple straightforward relationship begins to run into serious problems, however, with the contemplation of extreme velocities. In fact, as redshifts of higher and higher values were discovered, it was soon wondered just how long observers could go on breaking previous records. Eventually, spectral shifts were indeed measured which implied velocities of recession well in excess of the speed of light! Realizing the flat impossibility of such a conclusion, in terms of traditional physics and established views of radiation propagation, it became necessary for science to make so-called "relativistic adjustments" in order to reduce velocities to more plausible levels. Hence, while it is possible to measure comparatively large redshift displacements, the inferred speed of recession will be less than that of light.

The mathematical form of this adjustment may be stated as follows:

$$1 + Z = \sqrt{\frac{C + V}{C - V}}$$

Where:

C = Velocity of light.

V = Intrinsic velocity of recession.

Thus a receding source with $Z = .24$ will have its spectral lines displaced by some 24%; $Z = 1.00$ by 100%; $Z = 2.00$ by 200%, etc. Upon the basis of formula such examples will be seen to have true velocities of recession of some 21.5%, 60% and 80%, respectively, of the speed of light. (This relationship, between Z and velocity, is depicted rather precisely by the curve in Fig. # 4, where it serves to express the time of light transit in full accordance with the dictates of an expanding universe and the "law of addition of speeds.")

In making this very necessary adjustment of speed and distance, there is now reason to suspect that science has actually managed to adopt the correct formula while approaching the problem from the wrong direction, and in spite of using misleading logic in order to bypass the real issue that is involved! Instead of looking to the Special Theory of Relativity for an explanation (and entertaining only partially conceived ideas of increasing mass and slowing of time with rapid motion), the formula is really no more than a surreptitious reinstatement of the "law of addition of speeds" - a valid law of nature which was supposedly (and unjustifiably!) abandoned following an unfortunate misinterpretation of the Michelson-Morley light experiment toward the close of the 19th century! (Of truly immense importance to a proper understanding of many cosmological mysteries, this vital issue of light propagation will be discussed at length in Chapter 3.)

Quasars

Few discoveries by the science of astronomy have inspired more controversy than the detection of the first quasars back in the 1960's. Characterized by a range of unprecedented extreme redshifts, these peculiar starlike objects immediately posed both an enigma and a challenge for man to use them as distance indicators in his quest to map the far reaches of the universe.

The initial mystery hinged upon the realization that quasars are incredibly luminous for their sizes. If these extreme redshifts were truly indicative of great distances - in the sense that they implied enormous velocities of recession due to expansion of the universe - then their prodigious output of energy seemed incomprehensible in the light of contemporary physics. How could the energy-emitting region of a quasar, perhaps no more than a few light days in diameter, possibly liberate up to a hundred times as much energy as a giant galaxy containing hundreds of billions of stars?

Within a decade or so it was generally agreed that a supermassive black hole must somehow be involved if the inferred energy generation is indeed real. Rotating with extreme rapidity, the tremendous gravitational energy of a massive black hole is greatly supplemented by the dynamo effect of a powerful electric field sufficient to draw vast swarms of encircling quanta into intimate association. The outcome of such a dense concentration of swirling energy forms, according to recent theory, is a perpetual deluge of newly created electrons and positrons spewing from the vicinity of a quasar's black hole core. In any event, it is admittedly more than a little ironic that a supermassive black hole, from which nothing is expected to escape, should turn out to be responsible for powering the most luminous objects in the universe!

While a huge black hole dynamo might thus solve the energy problem, a few skeptics still doubted whether the major proportion of a quasar's redshift was really due to expansion of the universe. This was to be a matter of controversy for some years to come. An intense gravitational field, it had long been established, could also cause a redshift in spectral lines. The very act of attributing a supermassive black hole to the central regions of a quasar was, they were quick to point out, an open admission that at least part of their extreme redshifts might be of gravitational origin. (And yet, even this possibility was seen to pose a severe contradiction since, among other reasons, it would imply an inordinate amount cf spectral line broadening that is not in evidence with observation.) To compound the situation, instances were eventually found where some quasars seemed to be associated with galaxies and other quasars of widely differing redshift. Although subsequent investigation disclosed an abundance in the number of quasars far beyond original estimates - thereby increasing the probability of chance association - the question was never really settled to the complete satisfaction of all. About the only unanimous decision to emerge, during the early pioneering days of quasar research, was that many of them must surely lie at extreme distances - distances well beyond the confines of our own Local Supercluster.

More recently, evidence has been steadily mounting in support of the cosmological interpretation, which now appears to be quite firmly established in the eyes of most astronomers. Velocity of recession is, first of all, by far the most logical explanation for such extreme redshifts. Secondly, the finding of some quasars with spectral line displacements similar to those of certain surrounding galaxies - in full compliance with the Hubble law - is strongly suggestive of a common origin and location in space. A third indication arises from the fact that there are no quasars with redshifts indicative of distances of the order of our own super-cluster - a clear hint that separations well in excess of several hundred million light years are involved!

On the whole, and conceding instances whereby some quasars do in truth exhibit redshifts requiring a more subtle explanation, it seems highly unlikely that present confusion must negate all value as potential distance indicators. Typically a hundred times (or more) as luminous as a giant galaxy, with some modification of light propagation theory there is now every promise that these exotic objects afford the necessary means with which man may probe to the very edge of the universe!

THE ETERNAL UNIVERSE

Chapter 2

EVOLUTION AND REINCARNATION

(The Procession of Life - The Evolution of Man - The Mechanism of Evolution - The Pyramid Concept of Reincarnation.)

Although modern theories of stellar evolution and cosmology are only able to define broad limits with regard to the age of the Earth, there is fortunately a way to obtain a date which is more specific. In a sense, certain rocks constituting our planet's crust may be said to contain a sort of internal clock, one capable of running for many billions of years and remarkably trustworthy. These rocks contain radioactive elements such as, for instance, U^{238} (92 protons, 146 neutrons) and U^{235} (92 protons, 143 neutrons). These two isotopes of uranium have half-lives of 4.51 billion years and .707 billion years, respectively. The former decays spontaneously to an end product of an isotope of lead known as Pb^{206} (82 protons, 124 neutrons); while the latter ends up as the lead isotope Pb^{207} (82 protons, 125 neutrons). Inasmuch as the natural isotope of lead is Pb^{204} (82 protons, 122 neutrons), appropriate analysis of rocks containing these uncommon isotopes is capable of yielding a fairly reliable guide as to the time that has elapsed since their solidification. Utilizing this procedure, scientists are now reasonably certain that the Earth's solid crust was likely formed close to 4 billion years ago, which is in favorable agreement with that of both meteorite and lunar studies and a parent Sun of slightly greater antiquity.

Conditions on our planet's surface must have been vastly different in the very remote past. In particular, free oxygen is believed to have been a relatively scarce commodity, only obtaining its present abundance some billions of years later as a consequence of the eventual build-up of oxygen-secreting plant populations. Lacking an oxygen-ozone atmospheric shield, with which to cut off much of the ultraviolet energy of the Sun, intense radiation would have bathed the surface of the Earth to a degree highly detrimental to advanced forms of life. By remarkable coincidence, this is precisely what nature required in order to facilitate development of the earliest living structures! Even at this initial stage of evolution, one is caused to reflect whether fortuitous circumstances chanced to assist molecular chemistry - or whether it was really an intrinsic phase in some Purposeful Cosmic Plan.

The Procession of Life

As most people know, virtually all knowledge of ancient life stems from the finding of fossils. A fossil may best be defined as the remains or impression of some plant or animal that lived during a past age. This information may be in the form of a shell or skeleton, a specimen in a state of petrification, an organism almost completely preserved in such a substance as amber, or merely an impression of a footprint imposed upon a layer of sandstone, etc. However, it should be borne in mind that only a limited number of living creatures can be expected to die in a manner conducive to fossilization and, due to a variety of factors, only the very smallest fraction of these will ever be found. Thus it will be seen that we can never hope to derive a complete picture of all the myriad forms of life which once existed on the face of our globe. Only an approximate and very fragmentary sketch is possible, dictated largely by the relative abundance, structure, and particular environment of the different species on the one hand, and the rather slim chance of our happening to find a few scattered remnants of the less common species on the other. A reasonable idea as to the probable age of a fossil may be obtained simply by determining the age of the rocks in which it is found. (See Fig. #1 for the divisions of geological time and a sample of the life characterized by each era.)

The earliest direct fossil evidence of life is thought to be primitive types of microorganisms found embedded in rocks dating back as far as nearly 3.5 billion years ago, suggesting that little time was wasted once the Earth had cooled to the point where delicate molecular bonds could prevail. In addition to microscopic bacteria-like organisms, blue-green algae of a complexity not too dissimilar to that of certain modern strains have been uncovered in rocks from the Lake Superior region of North America. Dates ranging from 2 to 2.7 billion years have been assigned to these finds, which clearly indicates that the development of cellular organisms had already achieved widespread profusion at this distant age.

THE ETERNAL UNIVERSE

By the dawn of the Cambrian period, some 570 million years ago, a wide variety of marine life had become firmly established. Large numbers of trilobites, a sea-bottom inhabitant bearing some resemblance to a horseshoe crab, are found embedded in rocks of this particular time. Other common fossils include many types of mollusks, crustaceans and brachiopods. In fact, all major invertebrate phyla are fully represented at this stage of evolution. The advance to an internal bony skeleton is generally believed to have commenced at the beginning of the following Ordovician period, about 500 million years ago, as fossil remains of primitive vertebrates first begin to appear in rocks of this date. No trace of land life (plant or animal) is yet in evidence, as the sea continues to hold its exclusive franchise.

This state of affairs was to be rectified during the subsequent Silurian period, however, as certain forms finally commenced a transition from an aquatic environment between 450 and 400 million years ago. Elementary types of fishes also made an appearance at this time, achieving great diversification and prominence by the close of the following Devonian period, about 350 million years from the present. Paradoxically, while some species of early fish were able to develop external armor of solid bone, it was not until later that fish in general were able to turn their internal skeletons from cartilage into bone. It would seem that the more "progressive" amphibians, undergoing a simultaneous evolution, were able to acquire bony vertebrae before the fishes themselves. In any event, the Silurian period was characterized by a number of subtle structural changes in emerging life forms - including features which would one day provide a basis for the ultimate echelons of biological manifestation. Small fern-like plants and a variety of swampy growths were among the first vegetation to have stepped ashore, to be followed by an assortment of primitive insects, some of which resembled the centipedes and millipedes of today. The land was at last beginning to bring forth fruit.

The Devonian period witnessed the culmination of revolutionary changes that had begun millions of years earlier. Certain advanced forms of marine life managed to supplant their gills with an entirely new mechanism permitting them to take oxygen from the air: they developed lungs. (It is instructive to note that several species of lungfish, which can breathe by means of either gills or lungs, remain even today as a reminder of a past age when life was emerging from the sea. Such forms also began to convert fins into leg-like appendages, endowing its owner with the ability to crawl.) The great climax to all these elaborate and mysterious modifications, which had been taking place in the sanctuary of the numerous shallow inland seas and connecting waterways of this era, was eventually reached when the first amphibians successfully invaded the land. This new and higher life form possessed the ability to choose between a terrestrial or aquatic environment. In effect, the amphibians were now free to share the advantages and challenges of two distinct worlds - with this most recent acquisition virtually capable of opening the door to another universe!

Very noticeable changes occurred during the Carboniferous period, which began about 350 million years ago, and in the succeeding Permian period commencing roughly 70 million years later. Gigantic ferns, huge horsetails, club mosses, and forests of cordaites comparable in size to many of our modern trees, were all typical of this age of lowlands and hot, dense, tropical swamps. Since much of this profuse vegetation grew in extensive regions of swampy marshlands, large amounts of decaying matter were soon covered with water and, robbed of the oxygen of the air, eventually gave rise to deposits rich in hydrocarbons. Thus it is to the solar energy stored by the luxuriant vegetation of this distant age that we owe our deposits of coal and oil.

With the passage of time the amphibians were gradually superseded by a variety of reptilian creatures with superior size, speed, and advanced egg laying capability. Unlike their predecessors, whose eggs required constant immersion in water, they were able to produce eggs having a tough outer skin or shell which effectively inhibited desiccation. Only at this point could it be said that evolving animal phyla had truly severed the last remaining link with its aqueous origin. Appearing initially in the Carboniferous period, it was not until the following geological period that reptiles attained wide deiversification and dominance. It is of note that the fossil record of this era also reveals some evidence of archaic forms of pre-mammalian life, suggesting an ancestory for mammals dating well back to the earliest reptilian inhabitants.

Spanning an interval of approximately 100 million years (from about 230 to 130 million years ago), the Triassic and Jurassic periods account for some of the most bizarre fossil specimens uncovered to date. Often referred to as the Age of Reptiles, the size and structure of some of these creatures almost defy description. Unquestionably, the most publicized types comprise the group of so-called dinosaurs, certain species of which grew to monstrosities as great as 80 feet or more in length, 40 feet in height, and as much as 80 tons in weight! And yet, in spite of their enormous bulk, they possessed tiny brains out of all proportion to size.

The honor of being the largest of these prehistoric monsters goes to a group of huge herbivores frequenting the numerous swamps of this time. Brachiosaurus, Brontosaurus and Gigantosaurus are typical examples of this class of wading dinosaur, huge four-legged creatures with long swan-like necks and equally long and powerful tails. However, the most ferocious and fearful of these dinosaurs appears to have been a species known as Tyrannosaurus rex, a giant kangaroo-like reptile 50 feet long and standing almost 20 feet high. This monster was strictly carnivorous as his powerful jaws and long, knife-like teeth would testify. In fact, he could conceivably be referred to as a great engine of destruction - a task for which he was certainly well fitted.

In self-defense against such enemies a number of reptiles developed armor plate, with the result that some species were virtually walking fortresses of sharp, bony plates and spines. One notable member of the horned and armored dinosaur category was Triceratops, a heavy creature built something like a rhinoceros, only much larger, often reaching 20 feet in length. The head of Triceratops was embedded in a huge bony shield from which two formidable horns resembling sharp spears projected. A third but somewhat smaller spike extended from the vicinity of its nose. Although vegetarian in nature, when aroused it must have posed a most effective and deadly battering ram!

The Jurassic period featured the appearance of a new form of life, a variety of flying reptiles which are generally classified under the name of pterodactyls. These winged reptiles had no feathers like modern birds; instead, their bat-like wings were formed of massive folds of thin, leathery skin. In size as well as in minor details these creatures varied widely; some were no larger than a bat, while others had wingspreads equal to that of a small airplane! Judging by the structure of these larger pterodactyls, however, it is doubtful if their wing muscles were strong enough to allow them to fly in the manner of ordinary birds; they would seem to have been restricted mainly to gliding and soaring.

The suspicion that birds originated from certain species of reptile was remarkably confirmed with the finding of such fossils as Archaeornis and Archaeopteryx in rocks of Jurassic age. These creatures were a most peculiar combination of half reptile and half ordinary bird. Although their bodies seem to have been poorly covered, probably with little more than fringed or tufted scales, their wings and tail were unquestionably blessed with real feathers. Both of these early specimens were comparatively small, about the size of a common crow, and possessed typical reptilian heads equipped with rows of sharp teeth. But perhaps the most outstanding characteristic of all is to be found in the structure of their wings; for at the end of their wing bones projected several usable claws - rather striking evidence that their front legs had been converted into wings! One could hardly desire more suitable specimens to illustrate evolution between two so seemingly different groups as reptiles and birds.

During the subsequent Cretaceous period (about 130 to 65 million years ago) a number of very dramatic changes occurred. In the plant world such modern trees as willows, poplars, birches and oaks began to displace the ancient cycads and conifers. The hot, tropical climate which had hitherto prevailed over much of our planet's land mass now began to moderate, and the extensive swamps and lowlands underwent fluctuations and adjustments as the ground once more pushed upward in its most recent major upheaval. But the greatest surprise of all is to be found in the animal kingdom; for with the close of this period the seemingly invincible dinosaurs have literally vanished from the fossil record. Never in the course of geological history has there been such a swift and thorough extinction of established species!

This mysterious disappearance has been the source of considerable speculation, inspiring a variety of quite different theories. One proposal is that a nearby star exploded as a supernova, and that the ensuing radiation most adversely affected the largest forms of terrestrial animal life. Another idea would seek to blame it on an inability to cope with a changing environment due to climatic conditions. A more recent concept involves postulating an encounter with an asteroid-sized celestial body - from whence the Earth's atmosphere became so filled with dust and pollutants that the vegetation upon which the dinosaurs depended was seriously depleted. Perhaps, as some authorities have suggested, there is a very simple and instructive explanation relating to the emergence of the smaller but much more intelligent mammals. Was it, they hasten to ask, just a coincidence that the two events should have transpired at this same point in time? Could it not be a case of intelligence finally prevailing over sheer brute force? (The reptilian practice of abandoning their eggs to hatch by themselves, for instance, could well have proven a disastrous trait in an age which featured smarter creatures with a liking for unguarded dinosaur eggs.)

In any event, with the conspicuous absence of the great reptiles the tiny mammals were now free to multiply and achieve dominion. The mammals at the beginning of the Tertiary period (about 65 million years ago) were typically not much larger than a cat or dog; yet despite their size they represented an immense stride over the life that had preceded them. No longer are they vulnerable to relatively small changes in temperature and humidity, for their bodies are now covered with hair or fur and their blood is of constant temperature. In proportion to size the structure of their brain is on a vastly higher level. Instead of laying eggs and abandoning them to the perils of the world, as is the usual custom of reptiles, they bear their young alive. But what is even more significant, they remain with their offspring and take a definite interest in them; they nurse them and care for them until they are old enough to fend for themselves. A new era had dawned; a teachable form of life had come into existence, and with it had come the priceless advantage of learning by imitation and communication!

Over the course of millions of years the tiny mammals grew much larger and radiated into a wide variety of forms. Not all of these warm-blooded animals remained terrestrial, however, for just as a number of reptiles returned to the sea so did some species of mammal. If size is any indication of successful adaptation, then the whale would certainly seem to qualify, since he is by far the largest living creature. And yet, in spite of his fish-like form, there can be little doubt that the whale was once a terrestrial animal; for while he is now without legs a close investigation of his skeleton reveals vestiges of limbs (with five finger-like appendages) which have since degenerated to the point where they escape notice from the outside, but nevertheless are highly revealing from the inside. (It is interesting to note that vestiges of degenerated limbs may also be found in such a drastically altered creature as the python, a large snake, etc.)

By good fortune, sufficient fossils have been found to afford a clear picture of the growth and development of a number of species over a considerable interval of time. Chief among the mammals are the horse and the elephant. The history of the horse can be traced back about 60 million years, when it was roughly the size of a dog and a multi-toed animal suited for forest travel. Some 20 million years later it was a three-toed creature, with the middle toe larger than the other two. About 25 million years ago it was the size of a Shetland pony, and although it still retained three toes the two outer ones had so deteriorated that the weight of the body was now borne almost entirely by the much larger center toe. With the passage of a further 12 million years the fossil record reveals a virtually hoofed animal fully adapted to run on the grassy plains of this age. (Incidently, vestiges of these degenerated toes are still present today in the structure of a horse's foot).

The earliest known ancestors of our modern elephants first appear in rocks of the Eocene epoch in Egypt, where it was then a small marsh or river-dwelling beast little more than two feet in height. During the Oligocene epoch it doubled its size and succeeded in acquiring both tusks and a primitive trunk before finally branching out into a number of subspecies. By the middle of the following Miocene epoch certain of these descendants - called mastodons - stood some five or six feet high at the shoulder and had managed to migrate, by means of the narrow causeway which connected Alaska to Siberia at this time, to such distant regions as the American plains. Pliocene rocks contain the bones of the larger mammoth, which was similar in all major respects to our present elephants. Apparently the lower temperatures brought on by the Ice Ages served to encourage (and most remarkably, we might add!) the growth of a warm covering of hair, as the species of elephant roaming large areas of North America and Northern Europe by Pliocene times were all huge woolly mammoths. (The frozen and almost perfectly preserved remains of this creature have been uncovered in Alaska and in Siberian tundras, where they eventually perished sometime during the most recent Ice Age.)

The past history of the order of primates, which includes such animals as lemurs, gibbons, monkeys, apes, chimpanzees, and finally man himself, is not so readily ascertained since they are not especially numerous and not so likely to become fossilized. Nevertheless, in spite of formidable obstacles, a surprising amount has been learned. Fossil remains of tiny monkeys and lemur-like creatures have been found in rocks of Eocene date, as early as some 40 million years ago. Later rocks reveal increasingly larger and more varied species of primate, some of which bear a much closer resemblance to man than do the anthropoids living today. This fact clearly indicates that mankind did not descent from an existing species, and strongly points to a common ancestry somewhere back near the dawn of the Tertiary period.

The Evolution of Man

Among the earliest primates, qualifying as a direct (albeit, very distant) ancestor of modern man, could well be the genus known as *Ramapithecus*. According to scientific tests, involving the decay of radioactive potassium into argon, a specimen of this hominid found in East Africa has been dated at about 14 million years. The reduced size of his canine teeth, in particular, is thought to argue for a reliance upon primitive tools and weapons. In turn, this would imply the utilization of hands and a necessity to stand and walk, at least at times, solely upon hind legs - making it possibly the oldest known biped among the primates.

A somewhat later and much more human-like genus is that of *Australopithecus*. Fossil remains of this definite biped have been recovered from a variety of sites, notably South Africa and East Africa, with the Omo Valley find in Ethiopia being conducive to dating by the potassium-argon technique. This relatively specific method has yielded values ranging from almost 2 million years (upper strata) to over 4 million years for fossils associated with lower strata. Not only is there strong evidence of tool usage, but there are even indications that he may have been a manufacturer of crude implements. It is one thing for a primate to pick up a digging stick or club; it is quite another to fashion items involving manual dexterity and intelligence. Since wooden artifacts are highly perishable by nature, it is not surprising that an assortment of chipped stone cutting tools monopolize these early finds - impressive evidence that the Stone Age had indeed dawned.

Suspected by some authorities to be a later sub-family of Australopithecus, *Zinjanthropus* was discovered in the summer of 1959 in the Oldoway Gorge, Tanganyika, East Africa. Again, potassium-argon dating was capable of assigning an age, in this instance clearly revealing the new find to be well over a million years old. The specimen in question possessed features less apelike than the older finds, having a deeper and more modernly arched palate and a cheek curved almost the same shape as that of a human. Scattered about a related campsite, on the shores of what had once been an ancient lake, were a number of pebble tools of a form substantially more advanced than the earliest examples of Stone Age Culture.

While the African continent seems to have held a monopoly with regard to the oldest fossil evidence of primitive man - thereby implying that it may have been a main focal point of human evolution - this picture is soon modified with the discovery of more recent specimens. *Pithecanthropus erectus* (Java Man), believed by some experts to have an antiquity approaching 800,000 years, bears an even closer resemblance to present man and is now classified under the genus *Homo* - becoming, in effect, *Homo erectus. Sinanthropus pekinensis* (Peking Man), found in the depths of a Chinese cave, is thought to be nearly 400,000 years old. With a brain capacity not far below that of modern man, he was an accomplished tool maker and hunter. In fact, charred bone fragments and ashes indicate that, along with a more recently uncovered site in Hungary of about the same age, he was one of the first users of fire. Perhaps among the oldest of European finds, the *Heidelberg jaw* (Found in 1907 in a sand and gravel quarry near the German village of Mauer) is considered to be a Homo erectus type roughly comparable in age with that of Peking Man. Yet another at Nice, France, where evidence of large communal huts has been uncovered. Constructed of wooden posts braced with stones, they housed a small fire hearth. Not only has this site yielded a wealth of stone tools, but the impression of fur hides and even a human footprint was discernible to excavators!

Possibly an early form of *Homo sapiens* (the present human species), *Swanscombe Man,* found in a gravel pit to the south of the Thames River in England, has been given a date of about 250,000 years. Judging by the assortment of associated tools and other artifacts, including flints and charcoal remains of campfires, it is logical to assume that he was a successful hunter who likely enjoyed home-cooked steaks. Similar in a great many respects to the *Steinheim skull,* discovered in a gravel pit (of the same intergalacial age) near Stuttgart in Germany, both specimens appear to be good candidates as ancestors to later European Neanderthal types. Perhaps an even more immediate relative of this next evolutionary plateau (with a probable antiquity of between 100,00 and 200,00 years) would be a group known as the *Solo skulls,* a slightly later type of early sapiens from a valley of the Solo River in Java.

Neanderthal Man virtually dominates the fossil record of primitive man from at least 75,000 years BP (before present) to as recently as 50,000 or even 40,000 years ago. Deriving their name from the original find in a cave of the Neander Valley, Germany, this race of early man is revealed as a rugged breed of hunters who once roamed over a very substantial area of the world. Since the initial discovery a considerable number of similar fossil remains have been unearthed, with some notable examples being *Rhodesian Man* (found at Broken Hill, Rhodesia, the *Hopefield* and *Saldanha skulls* (South Africa), and the *Ma-pa skull* (China). Adept in the art of fashioning a wide variety of stone cutting tools and weapons, their hunting prowess was sufficient to enable them to bring down animals ranging from deer to mammoth and rhinoceros. They also appear to have reached the point of entertaining religious feeling, since the arrangement of some of their bones clearly implies a ceremonial burial. In fact, in an excavated Swiss cave there was even evidence that one group tended to admire (or worship) stronger animal life forms - placing the skulls of bears, in this instance, in such a manner as to invite interpretation as a shrine!

Once the age of an examined fossil falls below about 50,000 years, it then becomes eligible for dating by the carbon-14 isotope technique. Utilizing this superior method some rather specific dates have been established for a wide range of sapien specimens. Intermediate forms from late Neanderthal to modern sapiens, his eventual successor, have been found in a number of locations and tend to reveal a continuum with regard to both physical evolution and cultural progress. (The Ice Ages in Europe seem to have had a detrimental and isolating effect upon its evolving sapiens population, with the result that the fossil record of this entire region is deficient in transitional forms. In turn, this would account for the impression of European Neanderthal Man being rather abruptly replaced by what is essentially modern man.)

With an effective means of dating many otherwise uncertain finds, a deluge of information has become available concerning that interval immediately prior to the dawn of recorded history. In particular, the Dordogne area of Southern France, with its beautiful valleys and limestone cliffs (often honeycombed with caves), has provided much valuable insight. The Combe Capelle find, for example, has yielded dates of 34,000 to 25,000 years BP. The *Cro-Magnon* discovery in 1868 (since highly publicized and stereotyped as a race which succeeded Neanderthal Man), is dated between 25,000 and 20,000 years BP. In other caves of this region a wealth of artifacts have been recovered, ranging from quantities of awls and needles (used in the manufacture of clothing) to talented artistic displays. In this last respect, literally hundreds of colorful paintings have been found on the cave walls. Chiefly depicting animals with which they were acquainted, they are of such quality that they would do credit to many present-day artists!

Migration of certain members of the Mongoloid race, from Asia to the Americas, is believed to have occurred during an occasion when Siberia was linked to Alaska by a land bridge. Moving southward, it was merely a question of time until they inhabited the far reaches of South America. Sites of human occupation of about 24,000 years BP have been discovered in the New World, and include such widespread locations as the Canadian Yukon, Mexico and Peru. In truth, the ancestry of mankind is revealed to be extensive in every sense of the word - utilizing virtually the entire globe as a nursery, *and with his origin rooted at the very dawn of life!*

Invariably, the evolution of man raises a decidedly fundamental problem with regard to a popular religious viewpoint. Traditionally, the so-called Christian churches have vigorously opposed evolutionary theory in any shape or form, steadfastly maintaining a blind faith in a literal interpretation of the Old Testament account of creation. Over the past century or so this official attitude has experienced little change, even if the more enlightened members of their flocks have long since entertained grave doubts as to the wisdom of ecclesiastical authorities. Some theologians, unable to completely ignore overwhelming scientific evidence, have attempted to mitigate the situation by means of a compromise. In effect, they would begrudgingly accept the reality of evolution up to a point - namely, to the extent that man himself is not included in the overall scheme. (This highly arbitrary exclusion is necessary, of course, in order that they might retain what must be described as a bizarre interpretation of the Adam and Eve narrative, along with an equally bizarre Redemptionist doctrine requiring a mystical fall of man.) Although these misconceptions invite discussion at length (see *Higher Perspective*, by the author), it will be emphasized here that modern science and rational thought must be allowed to prevail over myth and unsubstantiated interpretation of ancient writings.

In addition to conclusive scientific evidence, confirming man's evolutionary heritage, there is also strong support from such sources as philosophy and common sense. From a philosophical point of view the fossil record is one of ever increasing complexity and intelligence. This is precisely the pattern needed to inspire contemplation of the dynamic principle of evolution - leading to the conviction that we must reside in a universe ruled by *Purpose!* Plain reasoning is capable of proving the evolution of man by the simple expedient of eliminating the sole alternative of "special creation." Other than by admitting the evolutionary premise of changing species, the absolutely staggering profusion of fossil entities can only be explained by postulating an *almost endless number of separate creations, extending over vast periods of time!* But if God be the Creator, why all the trials and tribulations and "experiments" before finally deciding upon creating the myriad forms of life existing today? In terms of "special creation" the whole affair is obviously preposterous. Evolution - *including that of man* - is capable of providing not only a far simpler explanation, but it is the only one which makes any sense at all!

The Mechanism of Evolution

How could such unbelievably complex biological forms evolve from a microscopic origin? It is unquestionably a miraculous feat, and one which defies adequate scientific explanation, but if we possessed the faith of a "grain of mustard seed" the phenomenon of evolution would be seen to be a relatively minor achievement. For nature demonstrates daily the evolution of life into exceedingly complicated structures. From a tiny seed may spring a huge and towering tree; from a single living cell may evolve a creature comprised of many trillions of cells; where there was once a lowly caterpillar there is now a beautiful butterfly. All of this not only takes place before our very eyes, but it does so without necessitating one act of "special creation"; for essentially, *evolution is the mechanism used throughout!* Since it is obvious that these everyday "miracles" could not have occurred as a result of chance, we must admit the influence of "anti-chance" - of *God* - an assumption which, incidently, also explains the overall success of evolution in spite of numerous monstrosities and blind alleys.

As most people know, all living tissue (plant or animal) is built around numerous tiny structural units called cells. The average cell is quite small, usually only a few ten-thousandths of an inch across, and so cannot be viewed except under a microscope. But in spite of their limited size, cells are exceedingly complex entities containing many billions of atoms, and possess inherent properties common to all higher forms of life. They can eat, digest, secrete, reproduce and, in some instances, have even displayed an ability to learn through experience; they are alive by all standards of evaluation! Certain types of cells, such as amoebae, protozoa, infusoria and bacteria, are essentially single-celled animals living on their own; while others live together in colonies ranging from a few cells to structures comprised of vast multitudes. (An ordinary housefly may contain as many as several hundred million cells, while man himself is estimated to consist of literally hundreds of trillions of individual cells!) Although all cells have many things in common, they vary widely in both shape and size as well as in their life functions. Thus the more complex organisms like man are composed of many specialized types of cells, ranging from skin cells, muscle cells, brain cells, bone cells, red and white blood corpuscles, germ cells, etc.

While a cell contains a number of other bodies, entrusted with a variety of functions, the nucleus itself is the center of organization and government. Within this highly significant region are elongated strands of a nucleic acid molecule known as deoxyribonucleic acid (DNA). Assuming the shape of specific threadlike spiral bodies called *chromosomes,* at certain stages of cell division, these structures hold the hereditary information essential for reproduction and for the overall functioning of the organism. In turn, the chromosomes are comprised of numerous tiny segments of intelligence commonly referred to as *genes* each of which may be thought of as a miniature "mind" or memory storage unit. Acting in conjunction with each other, these microscopic genes are able to produce a somewhat similar molecular substance named ribonucleic acid (RNA), which is able to move out of the cell nucleus and act as a "template" for the construction of the vital amino acids upon which life is based. On the whole, it may be said that the double helix pattern of DNA molecules - with their extensive strings of genes - is highly analogous to a linkage of the vast swarms of neurones (brain cells) so constituting our own brain! Indeed, the only real difference is likely one of mere *magnitude* - with these minute genes interacting together to manifest an overall living entity just as surely as our cerebral structure (of linked neurones) is able to give rise to a human mind or soul!

Thus it will be deduced that even the most elementary cell is a life form of incredible complexity, and one which could not have arisen from a lower level were its evolution not guided and determined by some intelligent force - *an intangible influence which must be ascribed to the presence and properties of spirit!* Moreover, the dynamic constitution of genes leaves little doubt as to their intrinsic nature: *they are simply aggregations of atoms housing or manifesting a degree of intelligence, or spirit!* And yet, the fact that such concentrations of matter do manifest spirit should not really come as a surprise; for after all, where there is life there must surely be spirit!

The means by which all living organisms have evolved into their present structures must be attributed to the effects of countless mutations. Insofar as evolution is concerned a mutation may best be defined as the failure of the genes, inhabiting a germ cell, to reproduce themselves in an exact manner. No form of life, even comparatively simple organisms like viruses and bacteria, is free from mutations, which appear to occur at random and are almost always harmful or useless variations. In general, changes of an advantageous nature are far too gradual to be observed over short periods of time.

But what, actually, are the changes that take place within the genes and chromosomes and which give rise to mutations; and what factor (or factors) are responsible for these changes? The structural changes which may occur are of essentially two kinds. By far the most frequent cause of mutations must be attributed to rearrangements, losses, or duplications of existing genes. However, from an evolutionary point of view, it is clear that constructive mutations are inevitably linked to internal changes within the constitution of the genes. Indeed, since no amount of duplication or juggling of existing genes could ever produce genes possessing different properties, and endowed with the ability to perform more complicated tasks, it is obvious that the remarkable course of evolution rests primarily upon *internal* changes in the atomic configurations of the genes themselves!

When one surveys the course described by evolution, with a seemingly miraculous transition from precellular life into unbelievably complex structures, can it be seriously doubted that *guidance* was involved? Surely, the almost infinite complexity of our very bodies is sufficient to convince us that we are not the product of chance! This is a conclusion which forces us to acknowledge that some "intelligent" factor must reside within the genes and, moreover, that it is the actions and influence of this factor (spirit) which is largely responsible for determining the course of evolution - essentially, the nature of a constructive mutation. What might appear to be a matter of chance must, in reality, be attributed to the work of some intelligent and immaterial factor - *ultimately, to the influence of that Cosmic Principle we choose to call God!*

It is rather strange that a materialistic approach has characterized so many attempts to explain the mystery of evolution. What might best be referred to as the "mechanical" basis of most current evolutionary theories may be summed up under the general terms of natural selection, adaptation, and so-called chance mutations. Upon such a flimsy platform purely random or accidental mutations are held to provide the raw material for the omnipotent and deciding influence of environment, which in turn is supposed to determine whether organisms possessing these new features will be allowed to live and to multiply. This process of weeding out undesirable and unfitted forms of life is known as natural selection or survival of the fittest, and as a result the surviving forms are said to be those which are adapted most suitably to their environment.

Now this is all very fine, and we must certainly admit that an adverse environment will tend to eliminate malformed and unsuitably adapted species; but when we attempt to apply such arguments to the problem of evolution itself we find that, in actuality, *we have a framework capable of explaining essentially nothing!* Not only must it be acknowledged that advantageous mutations rarely (if ever) arise through pure chance, but the very course of evolution is plagued with an almost endless number of instances which are quite contrary to the dictates of natural selection! For example, it must be apparent that in practically every phase during the transition of life towards greater complexity, rudiments of useless or even detrimental structures must have arisen. One might say that some mysterious providence *foresaw,* as it were, the usefulness or *later need* of many diverse and highly complicated structures! Obviously, traditional "mechanical" theories are misleading and wholly inadequate, since they fail utterly to explain the course of evolution.

But the initial and altogether crushing blow to the materialistic point of view may be traced to the appearance of the first life itself. *Where did it come from?* Indeed, where does this mysterious "spark of intelligence," representing the difference between life and death, continue to come from? For some unknown reason very few serious attempts have been made to incorporate the presence of *spirit* into a theory embracing evolution. Why this has been so constitutes a great mystery; *for does not all life - including our own soul - consist of spirit?* Furthermore, if we are to believe in the existence of a future life, and since there is overwhelming evidence as to the reality of evolution, we have no other alternative but to recognize the presence and interaction of spirit with *all levels of creation - from man down to the most elementary genecomplexes, and even to the ultimate depths of matter itself!*

A truly fundamental problem, which has long intriqued philosophers and scientists alike, is that of explaining the transition from inanimate molecular configurations to patterns characterized by life or spirit. When does a group of atoms cease to be inorganic matter and become a lowly form of life? Was the emergence of the first life on our planet simply a fluke of nature, involving a chance "fortuitous concourse of atoms"? Or, on the other hand, was it an inevitable result of dynamic properties inherent in the very constitution of so-called material particles?

Laboratory experiments have left no possibility of doubt with regard to the universal ability of atoms to engage in a spontaneous generation of organic molecules. Placing various common elements and simple inorganic substances in a flask containing water, and autoclaving the entire apparatus so as to ensure sterility, scientists have performed series of tests utilizing such energy sources as heat, electric spark, ultraviolet and X-ray radiation, etc. The results turned out to be both impressive and conclusive, as a host of organic compounds were readily synthesized - including many vital amino acids, nucleosides and nucleotides, along with the bases adenine, cytosine, guanine, hypoxanthine and uracil. In short, a wealth of complex organic chemical compounds is bound to be the rightful heritage of all newly formed Earth-like planets throughout the universe. The widespread evolution of biological life must, accordingly, be considered a foregone conclusion!

Conceding the inherent potential of matter to initiate life, the question remains as to how particular arrangements of atoms could give rise to intelligence. Not only do we have the level of microscopic gene-spirits and cellular entities to consider, but there is also the overall consciousness of the entire animal phyla - of which the human soul is only a solitary example - demanding similar clarification. Obviously, the whole issue hinges upon a structural positioning of atomic particles so as to form specific patterns conducive to the manifestation of spirit. Bearing in mind the intangible and non-spacial nature of spirit, it is perhaps useful to visualize this association with matter in terms of a "capturing" or "housing" hypothesis. That is to say, when certain intricate "fields of influence" have come into being, as a result of the formation of appropriate molecular configurations (each atom alone is characterized by a variety of mysterious electrical, magnetic and gravitational forces, etc.), such complex fields of influence could be thought of as attracting and capturing a level of spirit or life. Thus the intelligence of gene-spirits would be seen to arise from specific atomic-molecular patterns; while the overall personality of a unicellular organism may be interpreted as being due to the larger scale patterning of gene-type configurations. Upon a still higher plane, as more advanced animal forms are contemplated, the interactions of specific patterns of brain cells are able to facilitate the capturing of spirit of steadily increasing value.

In spite of a wild profusion of biological forms, over the lengthy course of evolution, there is clear evidence of *guidance* ever urging an upward development of life. This factor is evident at every major stage of diversification. In addition to explaining the miraculous construction of a multitude of exceedingly complex internal organs, which are totally inexplicable on the grounds of pure chance, this premise is borne out by a remarkable similarity in the external appearance of evolved forms. For example, one has only to look at the broad spectrum of the world's mammal population. Is it just a strange coincidence that virtually all such creatures possess one head, one mouth and nose, two eyes and ears, four appendages in the form of pairs of arms and (or) legs, five fingers and toes (or claws), etc.? Much rather can this parallelism be deduced as a striving toward some *ultimate goal* - namely, Homo sapiens, and beyond!

The highly diversified and somewhat haphazard path described by evolution can only be resolved upon the basis of *free will.* For it is solely by ascribing freedom of will to spirit that we are able to account logically for the numerous trials and errors of evolution. Failure to recognize free will as an intrinsic attribute of spirit is really tantamount to accusing God of outright incompetence in the creation of life! Imperfection exists in the universe simply because the many levels of spirit are less than Perfect - *not as a result of the direct actions of a Creator!*

Adopting this line of reasoning the outcome of evolution may be acknowledged to hinge upon *probability.* That is to say, a specific proportion of spirits can always be expected to utilize their potentialities and freedom of will in such a manner as to follow certain specified courses. Just as small-scale uncertainty of individual atomic particles gives way to large-scale stability when great numbers are considered, so nature has contrived to ensure the overwhelming probability that a minute (almost infinitesimal) fraction of spirit would pursue paths terminating eventually in man; while the vast majority could be relied upon to diverge and lead to the creation of an extensive chain of lesser species. Subsequently, the biological life pattern of our planet *may be likened unto the structure of an enormous pyramid* - extending from myriad swarms of gene-type spirits and virus entities to the present apex of modern man with his relatively small numbers!

The hypothesis of *Divine Guidance,* as the underlying motivation behind the success of evolution, admittedly places the entire problem of mutations and adaptation into the realm of philosophical deduction. But this in no way negates the validity of a concept. In fact, history is permeated with instances in which philosophy and logic have preceded a scientific explanation. Contemporary science, with its roots still embedded in archaic "materialism," is just in its infancy when it comes to comprehending *Cause* or *Principle.* For this reason it is sufficient to theorize the existence of a subconscious "feedback" mechanism between the gene-complexes of germ cells and the overall controlling spiritual entity. While the traditional view of natural selection may be expected to play a role in the adaptation of a species to its environment, it is also clear that the required mutations are - in some vital sense - most certainly *directed!* Comprised as our bodies are of several distinct levels of life or spiritual awareness, it is not surprising that one manifestation should have no conscious association with another. Indeed, it is as though quite different worlds are involved, with each being able to affect the other indirectly by means of diverting guidance or virtue received from above - *the ultimate source of which must originate in God!* (Again, a pyramid structure of the cosmos is suggested, with all virtue viewed as radiating downward from a point source defined as *Perfection!*)

Equivalent in many respects to that of conscience in man, employment of free will by the gene-spirits of germ cells must be held largely responsible for evolutionary mutations - producing both monstrosities (e.g., the dinosaurs) and the remarkably advanced life form now epitomized by Homo sapiens. This same principle also applies to the acknowledged ability of species to undergo environmental adaptation. What probably transpires, in such cases, is that *need* for structural change is capable of impressing itself upon the gene-complexes of germ cells. Exerting a "pressure" for appropriate mutations (if at all possible), the Darwinian concept of natural selection is then permitted to act upon advantageous variations. (Examples of this adaptive capability in man range from the increased resistance of some races to specific diseases, to differences of skin pigmentation in others commensurate with their exposure to sunlight, etc.)

Notwithstanding our present inability to grasp many details of biological evolution, it is both desirable and expedient to formulate one basic conclusion: *We must presume that the fundamental nature of the cosmos is such that all life contains spirit, and that it is capable of progressing to higher levels!* Only by making this most necessary and profound assumption can we possibly reconcile the idea of a future life with the reality of evolution. To think that man alone is the only spirit privileged to evolve to a higher status is absurd; for it is hopelessly in conflict with our

THE ETERNAL UNIVERSE

knowledge that even man himself originated from a lower form of life - *from a form far lower than the simplest cell, in fact!*

The Pyramid Concept of Reincarnation

A useful definition of the term *spirit* is perhaps in order at this point. Stripped of the often associated attributes of intelligence and memory, it may well be constructive to define the broad spectrum of spirit as *specific and varying segments of Perfection,* or whatever God consists of. In essence, a spiritual entity is basically a particular strength or *level of righteousness* - of a desire for Truth. It consists simply of a *degree of unselfishness -* nothing more! It is this feeling of *Universal Love* - expressed as a *level of reality* - which determines the actual status that a spirit is given, in the sense that the higher this level the more advanced its status with regard to the evolutionary structure of the universe. Thus it will be seen that spirit cannot possibly be divided into classes or categories. On the contrary, during the long course of evolution our planet must have witnessed a steady and unbroken procession of spirit of *gradually increasing worthiness or degree of Perfection. Principle,* in which spirit forever seeks to equate intrinsic worth with physical status, is acknowledged to be the one dominant cosmic feature - completely transcending such mundane characteristics as space and time should this be necessary to preserve Harmony and Justice. Once again, it will be emphasized that *no one spirit is able to progress to a higher state of manifestation to the exclusion of all others!*

These assumptions raise rather pertinent questions which have been asked by philosophers over the ages. In brief, why do we find ourselves born into an imperfect world? Why, in fact, should any form of life find itself situated where it does? If the universe is the handiwork of an Omnipotent and Perfect Creator, why is anything at all imperfect? What, in the last analysis, is the deeper significance of ascribing free will to spirit? Invariably, the entire issue must hinge upon *deservability of status* - in which spirit is seen to be not so much created as it is *constructed* in a lengthy step by step process from some infinitesimal origin. In order to acquire a higher nature a spiritual entity must *earn or deserve* this most cherished reward. Interrupted upon innumerable occasions by death, the evolution of a soul (or spirit) may only proceed on the basis of what might be described as the principle of *Cosmic Reincarnation.*

Actually, the many advantages inherent in the concept of reincarnation are extremely convincing. The old notion that we have but one all-determining life in which to prove ourselves worthy of passing to "heaven" is really seen to be quite illogical. For example, what happens to the soul of one who dies in infancy? Should we be so naive as to think that it passes automatically to a higher existence we are faced with the thought that those who live longer are unlucky, inasmuch as they have risked not making it, so to speak! Furthermore at what specific instant of time does a child cease being a child and become responsible for its actions? Clearly, no time limit can be established. A similar parallel exists with regard to adults. Who is to say that time will not lead to profound changes in one's spiritual outlook? And yet, we know that death shows respect for neither time nor person. Are we to relegate Divine Justice to the whims of blind chance, by failing to give all individuals an equal length of time and equal opportunity to evolve spiritually?

Upon the premise of reincarnation such objections will be found to have a simple and common solution. By acknowledging the reality of immortality of soul, or spirit, the time limit impasse is at once removed. The mystery surrounding premature death, or any death, for that matter, no longer exists since an appropriate rebirth will prevent the injustice which would otherwise ensue. To an increasing number of serious thinkers belief in reincarnation offers the only alternative to the spectacle of a chaotic universe. But what of the laws regulating this most dynamic principle? Can the basic theory itself be related to observational evidence? Unless this is done it must remain a concept embedded in mystery, despite its many obvious advantages.

Coexistent with the idea of reincarnation is the highly relevant phenomenon of evolution. Although feared initially (and still feared, in the eyes of many) as a materialistic doctrine by religious leaders in general, it was soon accepted by the scientific world as an undeniable truth. However, a major underlying reason for this rejection continues to invite more detailed clarification. Upon a philosophical basis, how are we to reconcile immortality of the human soul with the implications of evolution? If man really did evolve, from at least a microscopic origin, then where are we to draw a line as to the specific stage in which he suddenly became blessed with this great potential? Most certainly, precisely the same problem arises as must accompany any notion of one all-determining existence. A little reasoning is sufficient to show that the two are indeed connected, *and that the answer to the one difficulty is also the solution to the other!*

Rather than strive to impose a time limit where none may be imposed, or draw a line where none can be drawn, we are led to only one sensible conclusion. Without a doubt, it simply boils down to a case of *all or nothing* with regard to the issue of a life after death. Either *all* forms of life are eligible for a future rebirth, or else it is a false hope that does not exist at any level - including man himself!

Should we embrace the concept of a Just and Purposeful universe - in which all levels of spirit are capable of being reborn - the question of status becomes of paramount importance. For in order to justify its position, upon the evolutionary scale of life, a spirit must *deserve* the actual level which it is given. Accordingly, it can only deserve a particular status if it has had a *previous* existence! This leads, inescapably, to the conviction that all spirit must be traced to an extremely low and common origin - from whence the reincarnation process has since achieved wide diversification from the elementary gene-spirit entities characterizing initial life forms.

An extension of this assumption to the depths of matter is not without similar advantages in resolving the paradox of a Perfect Creator and an imperfect physical universe. As a matter of fact, considering that there is often great difficulty in distinguishing between animate and inanimate forms toward the lower extremities of life, any clear-cut distinction is frequently more arbitrary than not. It is, in reality, almost tantamount to attempting to draw another line where no line may be drawn. It may well be prudent, therefore, to consider even lowly matter to be of the essential nature of spirit - with the only genuine difference between life and seemingly inert matter being *one of degree or value!*

Upon reflection, the more one contemplates the validity of this concept the more logical it must appear. Matter has traditionally been looked upon as a lifeless commodity entirely divorced from such properties as mind or spirit. This view was all but demolished with the advent of modern physics, whose subsequent demonstrations of the interchangeability of mass and energy have left no doubt as to the fantastic power locked up in a **tiny speck of matter.**

THE ETERNAL UNIVERSE

Far from consisting of the "dead" substance that our senses would lead us to picture, matter may best be described as a composition of mysterious "forces" and "fields of influence" - quite in harmony with any dynamic motivation that might be ascribed to spirit.

Even the very concept of reincarnation appears to be in full agreement with a spiritualistic interpretation of matter, in spite of numerous instances of atoms and material particles being torn apart and fused together by circumstances over which they have no control. Invariably, the formation of new physical bodies must induce appropriate changes in associated spirit entities, in order that status (or degree of evolutionary progress) may again be justified. The process, in this case, is much the same as the phenomenon of birth and death in our own world. About the only difference which may be cited is that in matter we are able to detect the birth of new entities; whereas with the death of biological life we can see no direct proof of continued existence. It is surely a stroke of irony when the indestructibility of lowly matter may be adduced in support of the principle of spiritual immortality!

Proceeding with the fundamental assumption that spirit is capable of rising to immense heights from the depths of obscurity, we are at once confronted with an intriguing observation. It so happens, that the further one goes down the scale of life, the greater the numbers encountered of the lower spiritual entities. The difference in abundance of the various species of biological life alone is positively staggering - to say nothing of the vast multitudes of atoms comprising the simplest cell! *How could they all hope to evolve, individually, to higher levels?* For if these countless swarms of lesser spirits are blessed with the potential to eventually progress to the level of man (at least) - and they must be, since man himself is the product of a less than microscopic beginning - then does it not appear that only a fantastically small proportion could ever reach this advanced status?

There can, of course, be only one sensible conclusion: *We must deduce that many spirits of a low order may - in conformity to some dynamic law - be combined to produce fewer entities, but of a higher overall nature or status!* Solely by recognizing the principle of *fusion,* as a vital and integral cosmic feature, may we escape an otherwise absurd situation!

The mechanism of this inferred fusion process urgently invites detailed clarification. Meanwhile, there seems no compelling reason why we could not theorize a useful picture in harmony with the dictates of logic and observational evidence. (Inexplicably, the deep significance of this *fusion* principle has been overlooked by scientists and philosophers alike, with the result that a most important clue was missed - one which could have facilitated a much earlier solution to certain of nature's more treasured secrets!)

Let us begin by designating the lowest possible segment of spirit (or quantum of energy) as an "A". The least degree of fusion that it may enter into is union with another entity of like value. Should the two sufficiently deserve the resulting status they will surrender original identities in order to give birth to a new and higher overall entity, to which we might assign the symbol "B", of twice their previous individual worths. Similarly, the fusion of two "B"s could be visualized as leading to the formation of one "C", etc. The spiritual cosmos, upon the basis of such a doubling concept, might be viewed as a series of "steps" extending to higher levels of existence, *with each successive "step" containing an equal value of "A" but only half as many entities!* (So effective is this doubling process that a mere 100 "steps" is roughly equivalent to the huge sum of 10^{30}!) This is not to imply that the incidence of fusion is restricted to twofold jumps in status. On the contrary, there is every reason to presume a wide variety of intermediate complexes. For instance, the union of an "A" with a "B" must lead to the creation of an entity with a value of three "A"s. The fusion of a "C" with a "B" would result in a structure valued at six "A"s, etc.

Very frequently, in the oftentimes violent world of physical events, circumstances will produce an entity of a status undeserved by its recently fused components. In such an instance it must bring about the "death" - and subsequent rebirth - of the separate contributing entities, on the grounds that they are unworthy of the new status so created. Spirit of the appropriate level, itself the product of a previous disruption, would immediately inhabit the physical structure of higher value. (Time and space simply do not have any meaning to spirit temporarily lacking physical manifestation.) In this manner the ends of justice will always be served within the framework of a reasonable predetermined margin of tolerance.

By way of analogy our mysterious universe might be likened unto a vast pyramid, with rows of "steps" leading to its upper reaches. The base of the structure is wide, representing many entities of low worth, tapering steadily with height toward a point signifying fewer and fewer spirits of higher and higher value. At the top of this *Great Cosmic Pyramid* we have a peak or pinnacle which might be held to depict a state of *Maximum Fusion, or Oneness with God!*

Acknowledging that the basic principles of evolution and spiritual fusion must combine to produce a steady upward flow of spirit from lower levels, we may well ask where this dynamic process is likely to terminate. Regardless of the momentous and startling conclusion which must arise, no valid excuse can be advanced to predict an end to the evolutionary scheme only part way up the Cosmic Pyramid. This being so, we are left with no alternative but to recognize the *inherent right of all creation to rise to the height of Perfection, or Total Fusion!* For it must surely follow that, ultimately, *all spirit - man included - is destined to terminate in none other than God Himself!* Truth, or fusion into the One Body of God, is invariably our glorious Destiny! Therein is to be found both the Purpose and Motivation behind creation.

Chapter 3

THE NATURE OF GRAVITATION

(Gravitational Attraction - Gravitational Repulsion - Orbital Anomalies and the D/R Factor - A Revised Concept of Radiation Propagation.)

It is true, of course, that science has made considerable progress in uncovering the basic laws whereby gravitation exerts its influence, and also with respect to noting the curious relationship which exists between mass and energy. But in spite of the many experiences imparted to us by these forces it is evident that this knowledge concerns only effects; *the actual cause or motivation itself remains very much unanswered!* Why, for instance, should every particle of matter in the universe have an attraction for other particles? Why does the smallest amount of material contain an astonishing quantity of what might be termed "congealed energy" or "captured motion"? What, in fact, does energy or motion really signify? Proceeding upon the basis of spiritual theory there is reason to suspect that such effects are now capable of a measure of clarification.

Gravitational Attraction

Recalling that the very desire and destiny of all spirit - from the instant of its conception as a lowly "A" - is ultimate fusion into the One Undivided Body of God, need we be surprised to observe that a small spark of this inherent desire is manifested by every particle of matter? Essentially, what we choose to call the force of gravitation is none other than an expression of the *desire for spiritual advancement* which prevails at the more elementary levels of creation - of the constant striving to overcome an inferior and divided state by means of a literal fusion into fewer entities of higher value! Were we to seek confirmation of the principle of spiritual fusion, from the physical world which surrounds us, *no more graphic illustration could be provided than that posed by the phenomenon of gravitation!*

THE ETERNAL UNIVERSE

In order to separate unworthy and imperfect levels of spirit, and so prevent an unjustified fusion into One Harmonious Whole, nature has seen fit to introduce the basic property of distance. Such attributes of the universe as motion and energy are directly related and may, in fact, be looked upon as a further indication of a state of imperfection - *or absence of Total Communion!* It also follows that *rate of communion* is a factor to be considered in conjunction with distance and relative motion. Should interaction among components of creation be instantaneous, for instance, it would be equivalent to an elimination of both distance and time! Speed of communion is therefore seen to play a vital role in the overall scheme of cosmic events.

Conceding that gravitational interaction among material particles is actually a manifestation of such spirit's desire for communion (or fusion), the question of propagation becomes of paramount importance. Is this influence restricted to some finite velocity? Or, on the other hand, is it instantaneous in effect, and thus completely immune to all events which might otherwise be inferred due to association with time? Although obviously propagated at an extremely rapid speed, theoretical and observational evidence appears most implicit in substantiating the view that gravity is not instantaneous. Of all conceivable suggestions as to the velocity of gravitational communion, it would seem that the ultimate solution must center around the *speed of light* - clearly, a most significant and universal constant of nature!

With this thought in mind, and acknowledging the presence of vast swarms of unseen entities at the lower extremities of the evolutionary pyramid, we may now ask how the influence of gravitation is imposed upon bodies that are both relatively distant and massive. By what specific mechanism are particles of matter able to attract each other? Can we somehow utilize this impressive energy source which is presumed to exist in the form of countless minute quanta? While the basic concept of gravitational quanta - or infinitesimal bundles of energy - being exchanged by material bodies is not altogether new, the mechanics whereby this interaction is converted into a means of attraction has hitherto defied explanation.

A vital clue to this ancient riddle very probably resides in what has been termed *Newton's Third Law of Motion:* "To every action there is always an equal and contrary reaction." In short, what is implied in the case of gravitational attraction is that, whatever communion a body may receive from a source outside of itself, so it must promptly emit or relinquish an equivalence of such energy! (Were a material particle able to retain every quantum it encounters it would, of course, tend to grow infinitely greater.)

As a prelude to an attempt to resolve this problem, and giving due recognition to the principle of a constant exchange of energy among material structures, certain postulates may be stated as follows:

(1)　Gravitational quanta differ fundamentally from other material particles only in size or status, and may be described as elementary forms of matter which have yet to evolve - through the process of fusion - into more advanced structures. Consequently, in accordance with the basic premise that relative abundance is a factor of intrinsic worth, a wide variation in the status or mass of such quanta is bound to exist. That is to say, the lower the status the more abundant the structure.

(2)　Far from being instantaneous in effect, the propagation of such quanta is restricted to some finite velocity - essentially, a speed strongly focusing upon that of light itself. It may be presumed, in fact, that light speed represents *"escape velocity"* of infinitesimal quanta from association with some larger structure.

(3)　In general, when a typical material particle receives a quantum of gravitational radiation it will be unable to retain this additional energy and must quickly emit any surplus. Moreover, unless prevented by some infrequent occurrence, there will exist a pronounced tendency to eject this surplus in the opposite direction from whence it was received! In this event the inferred direction of emission is likely facilitated by the rapid rotation of the attracting body. Unable to penetrate the dense concentration of energy which constitutes a major atomic particle, a tiny gravitational projectile will be carried momentarily in the flow of this overall momentum. Finally, after rotation of the principal body has proceeded to the point where it no longer poses an obstruction, the newly acquired quantum is permitted to sever its association and resume its previous course with a final escape velocity equal to that originally possessed - namely, the speed of light.

(4)　As infinitesimal quanta approach within a critical distance of a material particle they will tend to come under the influence of an intangible force which might well be defined as anti-chance. The end result of this factor is to incite a greater influx of energy in the immediate vicinity of the material body, so that more quanta are received in unit time than could be explained on grounds of chance encounter alone! Such dynamic intervention may be ascribed, in principle, to the inherent desire for fusion which pervades all creation. As a consequence of this inborn desire, every particle of matter may be visualized as possessing a halo in the form of an encircling cloud of energy - an atmosphere of unassimilated and relatively minute quanta which is prevented from obtaining an unconditional escape due to the constant striving of spirit to secure fusion. Upon this basis it will follow that halo characteristics must be determined somewhat by the mass of the central body, in the sense that a more massive nucleus will exhibit a more extensive halo and be capable of retaining larger quanta.

Armed with the assumption that infinitesimal quanta are forever being absorbed and emitted by all material bodies, the task very much remains to relate gravitation with this exchange of energy. How is it possible to achieve attraction through innumerable encounters with these tiny quanta, acting as they must like a swarm of miniature projectiles?

Predictably, initial reaction to a larger than average flow of energy from one particular location in space - the direction of the most dominant mass - will be a slight recoil away from the point of greatest impact, as numerous high speed collisions serve to drive the body backward. Within the smallest fraction of a second, however, this motion of recession is terminated by the expulsion - in the *opposite* direction from whence received - of the excess energy just obtained. Acting upon the principle of jet or rocket propulsion this ejection will quickly return the particle to its original position. At this point the attracted mass will be made to oscillate rapidly with each cycle of absorption and emission, with the most conspicuous motion occurring along the plane of greatest interaction. The degree of this wavelike motion would be largely determined by the mass of the particle involved, in response to the logical premise that the more massive the body the less inclined it will be toward oscillation.

The key to the actual process, whereby small-scale oscillation is transformed into large-scale motion of attraction, would appear to reside in the production of what might be described as "neutral quanta." Just as swarms of infinitesimal projectiles may collide with bodies of much higher mass, so in regions of pronounced interaction numerous collisions must also occur among the gravitational quanta themselves. Following a collision of two such quanta there will prevail a brief moment when their respective motions through space are retarded or neutralized to a significant extent, or even cancelled altogether as in the case of head-on collisions among quanta of similar size! Considering that impacts of this type will be far more frequent in regions of concentrated mass, and especially along the plane of most intense interaction or exchange of energy, it will be inferred that therein exists a substantial supply of "neutral quanta" which an attracted body may absorb and convert into a means of propulsion. That is to say, when incoming and outgoing quanta collide in the immediate vicinity of some larger body it may then become possible to temporarily absorb this "neutral" energy into such a system - *without penalty of incurring a backward thrust in proportion to the energy received* - and thence to utilize this potential as "fuel" by reason of its subsequent ejection at the velocity of light! Thus the mechanism of gravitational attraction could well be explained through the acquisition of "neutral quanta" - *energy which may be absorbed into a system with reduced or negligible impact, but which is later ejected in the opposite direction at high velocity and with a recoil action sufficient to propel the particle in the direction of this source of energy!*

One important aspect of this proposal demands clarification. As an attracted particle is made to oscillate, through periodic absorption and emission of energy, it will follow that the strongest concentration of potential "fuel" must tend to lie along a narrow plane extending from the attracting mass straight through the center of the attracted body. But since the combined flow of outgoing and incoming energy will be the same on opposite sides of an attracted particle, it may be deduced that the frequency of collisions will be such as to produce as much "neutral quanta" on the side opposite the attracting mass as on the reverse side. Obviously, at this point, a successful interpretation of acceleration must hinge upon the acquisition of a larger proportion of this "fuel" from the direction facing the attracting mass. Unless this can be achieved theory will collapse of its own accord.

Invariably, this preferred assimilation is facilitated by the general flow of energy itself - a stream which flows most intensely in a direction from the attracting body toward the attracted particle. For one effect of this predominant stream must be to create a certain proportion of *secondary* collisions, as "neutral quanta" produced by earlier impacts are in turn struck by other members of this stream before they have had time to fully recover their momentum. Of fundamental importance, however, is the realization that when a secondary collision occurs between two interacting quanta the tendency will be to sweep this energy *toward* the attracted body! On the other hand, when such collisions are produced on the opposite side of the attracted particle, this potential source of "fuel" will tend to be swept away by the force of the prevailing stream, since the direction of flow is away from the attracted member! As a result, a high percentage of "neutral quanta" will be absorbed from the direction immediately facing the attracting mass. With the subsequent ejection of this "fuel," in a direction *opposite* to that from whence it was received, *the attracted body is thus enabled to propel itself toward the influencing mass!*

It now becomes desirable to assess certain properties of the halo, which is believed to surround all material particles, with particular emphasis upon the efficiency of the attraction process among particles of unequal mass. In short, will halo size and structure have any bearing upon the mechanics of gravitation? Both theoretical and experimental evidence would seem to leave little doubt in this respect, revealing that halo strength does indeed constitute a factor. Gravitational efficiency must surely vary with the mass of an attracted particle, to the degree that larger and more evolved structures, with their stronger and more extensive halos, will not respond so readily to acceleration as will smaller entities with more modest halos.

The explanation for this would appear to reside in the "insulating" properties of the halo itself. That is to say, a more extensive halo will serve to scatter or dissipate incoming quanta more readily than a smaller halo, thereby *insulating* the nuclear core from the "neutral quanta" that is so essential in achieving acceleration. For it is only when the thrust of ejected quanta can be imparted to the site of actual mass - such as the nuclear body that genuine work may be accomplished in moving the overall structure.

THE ETERNAL UNIVERSE

Hence it is to be noted that radiation in general can easily be boosted to maximum velocity due to favorable mass/halo relationships, while considerably heavier particles, such as electrons and protons, are more prone to squander energy and cannot be accelerated to this same degree. Protons, in particular, are noticeably more resistant to any attempt to push them toward speeds approaching that of light. In effect, due to the increased scattering of "neutral quanta" by a larger halo, only a relatively small and diminished proportion of this energy may be utilized by the nuclear body to secure acceleration.

Proceeding upon the aforementioned premises, it will be seen why an adjustment to Newtonian mechanics is required in order to express the factor of motion - simply because any external force must reflect the inability of gravitation to propagate at full efficiency when communion is limited to the velocity of light. However, rather than be misled by traditional relativistic notions of increasing mass with extreme motion, it will be acknowledged that it is really a case of *declining gravitational efficiency with increased relative motion,* as such movement makes it harder for quanta to catch up to rapidly receding bodies! Accordingly, at the speed of light itself the influence of gravitation must be virtually zero. The popular but highly nebulous idea of mass becoming infinite at light speed is both illogical and contradictory. (Indeed, radiation is propagated at just this speed and nobody has ever claimed infinite mass!) A modified relativistic formula, depicting a reduction of gravitational efficiency with increased relative motion, is illustrated in Fig. #2. (See also Appendix #1, which compares the efficiency of gravitation with the Z redshift adjustment of radiation. Yet another example of this principle is discussed in Appendix #2, which describes such phenomena as radio galaxies and jets.)

Gravitational Repulsion

Now a most important feature of gravitational theory is to be found in its "dual" nature. In actuality, *not all infinitesimal quanta may be exchanged in such a manner as to induce attraction!* As opposed to traditional belief, gravitation can no longer be viewed as an attractive force propagated indefinitely into space - one which merely "varies directly as the product of mass and inversely as the square of distance." For while this classical law is essentially valid within our Solar System, and may be applied with some measure of confidence to galactic phenomena in general, there is every reason to suspect that this is not the case when extremely large distances (such as exist between clusters of exterior systems) are considered.

According to theory the susceptibility of infinitesimal quanta to the influence of material particles hinges strongly upon the issue of size. In other words, smaller quanta will pose less of a challenge to a spiritual body attempting to exert its will - or desire for fusion - over other members of creation. (It is for this reason that the halos enveloping "maximum" particles, of the order of electrons and protons, are believed to be comprised of the more elementary levels of quanta.) Larger corpuscles must greatly increase the task of securing association and will, therefore, be far more likely to incur rejection. Nevertheless, even quanta too large to permit halo membership may be induced to follow trajectories of some curvature, in the sense that the more substantial the quanta the less affected their paths will be. Applied to the overall structure of an entire galaxy it means that the vast bulk of exchanged energy is caused to remain in circulation within the confines of that system.

But while the majority of ejected energy is unable to escape into the depths of outer space, it is also clear that this restriction does not apply to the more massive quanta. In fact, it is most logical to assume that a significant proportion of quanta - residing below the spectrum of light and radio emission - is indeed able to pass freely into space. Very conceivably, it could be the manner in which these larger quanta - escaping from clusters of galaxies - interact with the material particles of other systems *which holds the key to the observed expansion of the universe!*

Inasmuch as quanta of greater mass will (through sheer force) be capable of penetrating deeper into the halos of "maximum" particles, and so encounter regions of higher density or energy content, the result could well be a prompt scattering or rejection of this surplus - particularly toward the direction in which it is received! In effect, there will arise a situation whereby spiritual bodies are suddenly called upon to "process" more energy than they are capable of handling. As an injustice of this nature becomes more extreme, so it could demand a more immediate expulsion of such foreign quanta - quite regardless of whether they have had sufficient time to be whirled around to the opposite side of the principal body! Hence, in response to an injustice perpetrated against both host and invading quantum alike, an incentive will exist for the foreign body to quickly sever all bonds and rebound much as a ball will bound off a hard surface.

We may now see how an exchange of energy, among the various clusters of galaxies, could lead to a state of mutual repulsion and an expanding universe. For in the process of exchanging quanta, of a certain mass range, two distinct instances of repulsion will be inferred as this energy interacts with the major particles of such systems. In addition to the initial impact, which is a force directed away from source, there will be a secondary repulsive thrust as this undeserved quanta is swiftly rejected and expelled in the general direction from whence it came!

Since only a relatively small proportion of all exchanged quanta will so interact as to induce repulsion, it follows that inherent repulsive characteristics will be entirely masked by the predominant tendency to induce a state of "localized" attraction. On the whole, this universal exchange of energy may be viewed as a simultaneous existence of two opposing forces - with the force of attraction simply being the stronger at more moderate distances. With contemplation of the separations between clusters of galaxies, however, the hitherto dormant factor of repulsion is finally permitted to gain the upper hand, as the only quanta capable of being exchanged over such distances are the larger corpuscles which must act to induce repulsion!

This "dual" concept of gravitation, incidently, seems just what is needed to resolve a curious mass discrepancy involving clusters of galaxies. Astronomers of the 20th century were puzzled to find large inconsistencies in calculating the total masses of such associations by two different methods. One procedure, known as the "virial theorem" technique, depends on measuring the motions of member galaxies and relating this information with the principle that speed - within a gravitationally bound system - is a factor of mass. Alternatively, by computing the individual masses of the star systems comprising a cluster, simple addition will yield a reasonably accurate value. Invariably, a most disconcerting discrepancy arises upon comparison of the two methods. It was found that the kinetic energy of the galaxies implied masses far beyond that revealed by a more detailed determination of separate masses. Moreover, it was noted that the larger the cluster the greater this "surplus" motion which seemed to demand interpretation as excessive overall mass. This strange paradox has persisted in spite of careful investigation - presumably, serving notice that something may be going seriously awry when traditional views of gravitation are extrapolated to really large distances!

Recognition of a long-range repulsive factor, as an integral feature of a universal exchange of infinitesimal quanta, affords a most plausible explanation of this dilemma. At distances which separate cluster members the usual overwhelming aspect of gravitational attraction is greatly weakened. Accordingly, while still overshadowed, the repulsive side of this energy exchange is permitted clear expression. There will exist, in fact, a pronounced tendency for the constituents of a cluster to push each other apart. Prevented from doing so by a superior binding force, this energy must reveal itself in terms of enhanced galactic motions! In short, it is translated into the "surplus" kinetic energy which appears to undermine any overall mass determination. It is surely no accident that the magnitude of this discrepancy, which is generally a factor of 10 to 20, reflects the size differential between the diameters of the galaxies and the distances separating cluster members!

Upon the basis of a finite physical universe - and only a universe of finite dimensions - this underlying repulsive influence will be given an opportunity to express itself in rather dramatic fashion. Since nothing will be held to exist beyond the outer edge of the universe which would exert an inward pressure upon nearby clusters of galaxies, it may be deduced that the outermost clusters will be free to utilize this repulsive force to the full. Moreover, once started any outward movement must be cumulative in effect, in the sense that a recession of the outlying systems will reduce the normal inward pressure upon the more central members - thereby permitting them to share this large-scale motion without loss of efficiency. Thus the universe will be caused to expand at a constant rate, and in full agreement with the Hubble distance/velocity relationship which holds that the speed of recession is a direct factor of distance; that is, a twofold increase in separation will be reflected in terms of a twofold acceleration in velocity of recession.

Yet another indication of this "dual" nature of gravitation may well be found much closer to home - in fact, within the very confines of our Solar System! Ever since the orbits of the planets Uranus and Neptune became known with precision, it was realized that they did not quite follow predicted paths. Until 1978 it was assumed that Pluto, the outermost planet, was responsible for pulling them from their prescribed orbits. However, with the discovery of Charon, as a satellite of Pluto, it was possible to make a more detailed calculation of the mass of this system - revealing that there was no way in which these tiny bodies could account for observed perturbations. This surprising revelation has inspired a search for "missing mass" - ostensibly, in the form of a distant dark star or black hole. It will now be acknowledged that a hitherto unforeseen alternative exists - namely, *that the repulsive aspect of gravitation is at the root of this mystery*! Indeed, a measure of confirmation is already at hand in evidence afforded by the spacecraft Pioneer 11 (now well beyond Pluto) and its twin, Pioneer 10 (even further away at the other side of the Solar System.) To date, *no undue variation in their paths has been detected!* Were there an unseen body pulling at Uranus and Neptune it would almost certainly have revealed its presence by this time. Accordingly, the concept of gravitational repulsion emerges as the only viable explanation!

Upon due consideration of a possible formula, with which to describe this repulsive attribute of gravitation, it seems likely that the solution lies in ascribing a *twofold increase of repulsion for every fourfold increase of distance*! Radiating from the immediate vicinity of elementary particle nuclei, as a negative force some 10^{20} times weaker than the positive influence of gravitation, it may be presumed to increase with separation as stated - becoming equal to that of attraction at a distance of roughly 17 million light years. What is so very remarkable about this distance/repulsion (D/R) factor is the excellent agreement of all initial calculations with observation at such crucial test distances as those which characterize galactic cluster members, galactic extremities and halos, and the outer constituents of our Solar System. (At the distance of the planet Neptune from the Sun the inferred repulsion is about 192,700 times weaker than attraction.) In every instance there would appear to be strong confirmation of the implied degree of repulsion! (See Fig. #3 for a depiction of this D/R relationship.)

Additional evidence in support of this D/R aspect of gravitation may be found in the "bubble-like" arrangement of galaxies that

THE ETERNAL UNIVERSE

has recently become apparent. (See: "A Slice of the Universe," *The Astrophysical Journal Letters,* March 1, 1986.) Contrary to widespread belief, which would hold gravitation to be solely an attractive force, most galaxies are so distributed as to suggest an opposing influence; for they tend to reside toward the edges of "shells" or "bubbles" - with near voids at their centers! *This is precisely the pattern to be expected should gravitation manifest a "dual" nature!* Indeed, this observation is quite incomprehensible in terms of traditional cluster dynamics, which should feature central condensations of mass - not the reverse situation with such regions almost devoid of galaxies!

Orbital Anomalies and the D/R Factor

The inferred D/R factor of gravitation, which promises to resolve a host a "missing mass" problems, may well cast light upon certain instances of orbital peculiarities. Not only is there reason to suspect that the outer members of our Solar System are affected by a hitherto unforeseen repulsive component of gravitation, but impressive evidence exists that this same factor is responsible for a number of binary star anomalies. Moreover, even the much publicized perihelion advance of the planet Mercury must warrant further examination. A discussion of the D/R factor, as it applies to such phenomena, follows:

Mercury

By the dawn of the 20th century it had been discovered that Mercury did not exactly obey Newtonian mechanics of gravitation. After making due allowance for the influence of known planetary bodies, which were calculated to impose a perihelion advance of 531 arc seconds per 100 years, astronomers were puzzled to observe a rotation of some 574 seconds of arc. With failure to find a gravitational explanation in the form of an unseen planet, the mystery was presumed solved upon the basis of Einstein's theory of relativity, which was claimed to supply the missing 43 seconds of arc by reason of the following formula:

$$\frac{24 \times \pi^3 \times A^2}{T^2 \times C^2 \times (1-E^2)}$$

Where:

A = major semi-axis of the ellipse (57,900,000 km)
T = planet's period of revolution (87.97 days or 7,600,608 sec.)
C = velocity of light (299,784 km per sec.)
E = eccentricity of orbit (.206)
NOTE: The above formula is reputed to give the angle of perihelion advance (in radians) to be expected in one revolution.

For the planet mercury we may therefore derive the following angle of fractional advance per revolution:

$$\frac{24 \times 31.0063 \times 3.3524 \times 10^{15} \text{ km}}{5.7769 \times 10^{13} \text{ sec} \times 8.987 \times 10^{10} \text{ km/s} \times .9576} = 5.0179 \times 10^{-7}$$

Since one radian contains 57.296 degrees (or 206,265 arc seconds), it will be deduced that 206,265" x 5.0179x10-7 = .1035 arc seconds of advance per revolution. Inasmuch as Mercury makes 4.15 revolutions per year, in 100 years there should be .1035" x 415 or 42.95 arc seconds of advance - a figure seemingly in full agreement with observation. However, as has been aptly pointed out by more than one critic, this formula was devised for the specific purpose of yielding just such an answer. It is one thing to produce an equation giving desired results; it is quite another to explain all the intracies involved in a complex relationship for which only a partial understanding exists!

Utilizing a formula which rather directly describes the declining efficiency of gravitation with increased motion, we may calculate this velocity effect for Mercury (as a fraction of the Sun's gravitational influence) as follows:

$$I = \left(M \div \sqrt{1 - \frac{V^2}{C^2}}\right) - 1 \quad \text{or:} \left(1 \div \sqrt{1 - \frac{48^2 \text{ km/s}}{299,784^2 \text{ km/s}}}\right) - 1 = 1.3 \times 10^{-8}$$

THE ETERNAL UNIVERSE

The number of arc seconds traveled by Mercury in an interval of 100 years = 360 x 60 x 60 x 4.15 x 100 = 5.3784×10^8. Subsequently, the angle of advance to be ascribed to reduced efficiency of gravitation, in a period of one century, will be 5.3784×10^8 arc sec x 1.3×10^{-8} = about 7". Upon subtracting this amount from the missing 43" we are left with some 36" still to be accounted for. (It will be noted that reduced gravitational efficiency - due to motion - acts to delay the point of closest approach, thereby causing the perihelion to advance.)

Paradoxically, the D/R factor can serve to *both advance and retard perihelion!* In the process of exerting a "push," away from an interacting body, it will reduce the strength of gravitational attraction - imposing yet another instance of perihelion advance. On the other hand, the very action of imparting thrust must also increase orbital distance and extend transit time - in effect, retarding any advance of perihelion. The problem is therefore seen to be one of assessing the relative value of these two opposing influences.

According to the dictates of the proposed D/R relationship, the factor of repulsion at Mercury's average distance of some 5.7893×10^7 km will be 5.362×10^{-7} times that of the Sun's gravitational attraction. In terms of the Sun's ability to induce 5.3784×10^8 arc seconds of travel per century, it is equivalent to 5.3784×10^8 arc/s x 5.362×10^{-7}, or about 288.4 arc/s per 100 years. Thus, by way of a somewhat simplified explanation, the unaccounted for 36" perihelion advance may be resolved upon the premise of about 56.25% (162.2") of the D/R energy serving to advance and some 43.75% (126.2") acting to retard perihelion.

DI Herculis

One highly relevant example of an eclipsing binary star system that has been studied in some detail is DI Herculis, two main-sequence stars with similar physical attributes and a combined mass almost ten times that of our Sun. Orbiting a common center of mass in a period of 10.55 days (or 34.62 orbits per year), their separations range from 14,959,000 km to 44,878,000 km, with an average separation of 29,918,500 km. The observed periastron advance is some .65 degrees per century, with an uncertainty of ± .18 degrees.

As determined by Einstein's aforementioned relativistic formula, the periastron advance is a large 2.34 degrees per century. In addition, Newtonian mechanics imply a further advance of the order of 1.93 degrees per 100 years, making a combined total of some 4.27 degrees - a figure almost seven times higher than what is actually observed!

Application of the prescribed velocity formula, depicting a reduction of gravitational efficiency with increased motion (expressed in terms of exchanged energy), yields the following:

$$1 = \left(M \div \sqrt{1 - \frac{V^2}{C^2}} \right) - 1 \ \text{or} \ \left(1 \div \sqrt{1 - \frac{180^2 \ km/s}{299,784^2 \ km/s}} \right) - 1 = 1.82 \times 10^{-7}$$

The number of degrees traveled by each component in the span of 100 years = 360 x 34.62 x 100 = 1,246,320. Hence the angle of advance, which may be attributed to such a velocity effect in one century, will be 1,246,320 degrees x 1.82×10^{-7} = .23 degrees.

Simplified analysis of the D/R factor, as it applies to the system of DI Herculis, appears capable of supplying much of the missing .42 degrees of advance. At an average distance of 2.992×10^7 km, the inferred repulsion factor is some 4.47×10^{-7} times that of attraction. Expressed in terms of angular motion, we may derive the following result: 1,246,320 degrees x 4.47×10^{-7} = .56 degrees per century, of which a portion will serve to advance and the remainder to retard periastron.

Still to be considered, however, is an advance of 1.93 degrees implied by Newtonian mechanics due to periodic distortion of stellar bodies by gravitation. But since strong rotary motions of close binary components must act to generate tidal effects which vary somewhat according to their orientation, and in light of the D/R factor, it follows that much of this energy could be exchanged in a manner conducive to retardation - leaving only a small surplus to induce periastron advance. * In this particular case it is most logical to presume a distribution of energy very similar to that of the planet Mercury.

THE ETERNAL UNIVERSE

This entire line of reasoning can be put to an interesting test. If we add our .56 degree D/R figure to that of the 1.93 degrees, derived from Newtonian physics, we have a total of some 2.49 degrees. Application of the same ratio of advance and retardation, as indicated on behalf of Mercury, yields the following information: 1.40 degrees of advance minus 1.09 degrees of retardation = .31 degrees of advance. Upon adding this .31 degrees to the .23 degrees already inferred as a consequence of motion, we have the sum of .54 degrees of periastron advance per century - in very favorable agreement with observation!

Uranus and Neptune

Ever since the mass of Pluto was shown to be far too small to account for noted perturbations in the orbits of Uranus and Neptune, astronomers have been tempted to seek an explanation in the form of a distant unseen body orbiting beyond the known boundary of our Solar System. Upon the basis of a recent determination (Dr. Robert S. Harrington, *Astronomical Journal,* October 1988), the degree of perturbation is equivalent to a planetary body of some four Earth masses circling the Sun once every 1,019 years at an average distance of 101 astronomical units. (An astronomical unit is the mean distance of the Earth from the Sun.) It will now be seen that an alternative to this hypothetical Planet X exists in the form of the proffered D/R factor.

At the orbit of Neptune, a distance of 30.1 astronomical units (A.U.), the implied repulsion will be about 1 part in 192,700 (or 1.728 Earth mass) in terms of the Sun's gravitational attraction. With regard to Uranus, at 19.2 A.U., repulsion is roughly 1 part in 240,400 or 1.385 E (Earth mass). The amount of perturbation to be expected, upon the premise of our D/R factor, will be the difference between these two values, or a force equal to about .343 E. A rather

---

*The spin axes of close binary star members (relative to each other and to the plane of their orbits) can serve to regulate any periastron advance/retardation. Like rotation must generate repulsive magnetic fields which will reduce gravitational efficiency - leading to periastron advance. Conversely, opposed rotation among components is bound to give rise to magnetic fields conducive to attraction and increased efficiency of gravitational communion - resulting in periastron retardation. Thus it follows that, in the case of very close fast spinning binary pairs, the ratio of exchanged energy may well differ from the scenario of the more widely separated DI Herculis system - perhaps, even to the point of inducing occasional instances of retrograde periastron motion!

simplified but useful analysis of this entire perturbation scenario follows from a comparison of theorized D/R energy with that of calculations involving Planet X.

According to observational evidence the gravitational strength of any Planet X (relative to the Sun's attraction of 333,000 E) is equal to .867 E at Neptune's closest approach; while this same force is only .233 E when Neptune is most remote in its orbit at the other side of the Sun. The average influence is thus seen to be some .550 E. Similar computation for Uranus yields a figure of .238 E at point of closest approach, and .144 E at greatest separation. The average attraction imposed by this alleged Planet X, in the case of Uranus, is therefore deduced to be roughly .191 E. The difference between these two averages, which is determined to be of the order of .359 E, may be considered to reflect a reasonable assessment of noted perturbations. *Clearly, a most remarkable agreement is revealed to exist with regard to theory and observation!* It is, in fact, one more triumph on behalf of the proposed D/R factor.

Galactic Spiral Structure

Yet another instance of orbital anomalies may well involve a large-scale effect associated with the formation (and preservation) of spiral structure in galaxies. Considering that extremities of elliptical systems take much longer to complete a revolution about a galactic center than do the innermost regions, it has been wondered how spiral arms could persist after a few orbits. The very fact that such structure is so common among galaxies is a clear indication that some subtle force is at work upon a long term basis. By far the most promising theory to be advanced is a density-wave hypothesis, in which a rotating shock wave plays a major role in compressing interstellar gas and dust into regions of new star formation - producing luminous spiral arms. An essential requirement of this scenario is a pattern whereby matter is assumed to describe elliptical orbits about a galactic nucleus, with each successively smaller orbit offset relative to outer ones and in the same direction as the overall rotation of the system. A lingering problem, however, has been one of defining the actual mechanism capable of inducing this prescribed systematic alignment of orbits.

In essence, we are probably dealing with exactly the same set of circumstances responsible for the perihelion advance of Mercury and periastron advance of DI Herculis. Although upon a vastly larger scale, there is every reason to suspect that the existence of galactic spiral structure is intimately bound up in orbital peculiarities related to a declining efficiency of gravitation with increased motion, and in full compliance with the dictates of the aforementioned D/R factor. Indeed, a general precession of orbits must be the inevitable outcome of any reduction in the efficiency of gravitational attraction, regardless of how it is accomplished.

Most assuredly, the many implications inherent in the principle of gravitational repulsion invite urgent and serious investigation of a wide range of celestial phenomena. (Unfortunately, this is a concept unlikely to be welcomed by all members of the scientific community. With an alternate explanation for our expanding universe - in the form of steady pressure from within - there is bound to be resistance from many proponents of the Big Bang cosmology who would see their credibility threatened!)

A Revised Concept of Radiation Propagation

A number of revolutionary conclusions must arise as a result of our new interpretation of gravitation. The hitherto unresolved "wave" aspect of radiation, for instance, now promises to shed much of its mystery. We can readily understand why the various material particles exhibit wavelike characteristics, as they are caused to oscillate through periodic absorption and emission of minute gravitational quanta. But can we adopt this same principle to account for the rhythmic wave movement of radiation as it streaks through space? Considering such a phenomenon as the polarization of light it soon becomes evident that a more subtle explanation is in order.

By far the most logical solution would seem to involve the view that radiation does not normally consist of individual corpuscles. Just as many stars are members of double systems, so it may be expedient to visualize radiation as primarily miniature *binary systems* - essentially, two entities revolving about a common center of interaction while yet moving through space as a unit. (Polarized light may be explained as swarms of minute binary systems possessing a specific and common orientation in space.) Due to this rotary motion a quantum of radiation will be observed to display a spiral or "wave" trajectory, with the particular wavelength itself simply requiring interpretation as an *expression of the degree of separation of the binary components!* (It will be understood, of course, that the actual separation between such members is not synonymous with the distance from one wave crest to the next, as the latter attribute is really a measure of how frequently the components complete their mutual orbits. Since orbital speed decreases with either reduced mass or increased separation of the system, in full conformity to established laws of motion, it follows that more massive and energetic components will be closer together and hence able to complete more orbits in unit time - signifying shorter wavelengths - than more widely separated members of smaller mass.)

In view of the obvious simplicity of the concept, and considering its ability to clarify an otherwise baffling situation, it may be wondered why science ever hesitated to adopt this picture of the wave-particle duality of radiation. The most conspicuous objection is one which even threatens to ridicule the very suggestion (especially when we contemplate radiation of higher wavelengths), since it involves the apparent lack of an attractive force sufficient to retain the structure of such weak systems. For example, when we consider that most binary components would have to be assigned separations exceedingly vast by nuclear standards, it may indeed be asked why these associations are not immediately disrupted by much closer relationships with far more massive and influential particles.

Upon the basis of a limiting velocity on behalf of gravitational interaction (e.g., the speed of light), and with a knowledge of how acceleration is accomplished, it will now be seen that by the time full communion could be established with any nearby material particle a tiny bundle of radiation *will have left that particular region of space* and will, therefore, be largely unaffected! (Invariably, a direct hit or exceptional near collision would be quite another matter.) Thus, by reason of a common motion through space which would permit a state of mutual communion to exist, a binary system of minimal gravitational attraction may be constructed - *providing that this system possesses the velocity of light relative to any body which might tend to disturb it!*

Having introduced a proposal whereby material particles may

achieve attraction, it now becomes necessary to explore the laws regulating this acceleration. What, for instance, prevents acceleration of a body beyond the velocity of light? As a matter of fact, when we talk in terms of velocity it may well be asked what is really meant. To what specific point is any motion relative? If the speed of light represents some limiting velocity, then it is at once evident that a body possessing this "maximum" velocity relative to one system will not possess this same speed with respect to all other moving systems. Two light photons traveling in opposite directions will obviously exceed the speed of light relative to each other. Likewise, clusters of galaxies clearly exist which display combined velocities of recession in excess of this speed. Hence, in a broad sense, the velocity of light can be surpassed and any inferred restriction very much remains to be concisely stated.

Essentially, the speed of a body through the medium of space is regulated by its ability to acquire "neutral quanta," with acceleration proceeding just as long as it is possible to obtain and utilize such propulsive "fuel" to advantage. Should we theorize motion in excess of the speed of light, energy encountered in the direction of flight will actually strike with greater force than the recoil action with which it is later ejected - thereby constituting a braking action! Also sharply curtailing acceleration at extreme speeds is a drastic reduction in the receipt of "neutral quanta," since the only effective mechanism with which to slow the approach of incoming quanta - in the line of flight - involves collisions with other quanta traveling in much the same direction as the body itself. But if a body is moving - relative to the prevailing gravitational field - at a speed close to that of light, it is evident that only a minimal amount of quanta could ever manage to catch up to it from behind in order to retard the momentum of the oncoming quanta! Thus, at speeds approaching that of light, the issue of particle acceleration is seen to hinge upon the very marginal assistance of quanta arriving from a direction opposite to that in which the body is moving. It is for such reasons that velocity becomes so crucial at extreme speeds, and which accounts for the self-terminating aspect of acceleration once the velocity of light is attained relative to the prevailing gravitational influence.

In assessing all aspects of acceleration it will be noted that any adjustment of speed is the joint product of both velocity and density of the medium through which passage is attempted. In a sense, extended motion through a tenuous gravitational field is really equivalent to a shorter encounter with an intense field. Nevertheless, it is most essential to understand that *it is the actual velocity of a body which becomes of overwhelming importance at extreme speeds!* For as the velocity of light is approached the chief effect of a stronger gravitational field will be to merely expedite any required adjustment of speed - *an adjustment which the weakest field will surely facilitate, even if it should take a slightly longer period of time!*

Certain consequences of extreme motion warrant discussion. It may be inferred, first of all, that a body moving through a gravitational medium at close to the velocity of light will exhibit an increase of mass due to the greater volume of quanta swept up and momentarily detained, where it must add to the strength of the halo - additional quanta which, for all practical purposes, must be viewed as intimately associated with the body in question. Reduce the strength of the prevailing field and this ability to increase mass through motion will also be reduced. But rather than be misled by a popular analogy, which would tend to visualize mass as being increased by an infinite amount once the velocity of light is attained by a material body - an obvious impossibility - it will simply be acknowledged that as this speed is approached, and more quanta encountered, so an enhanced proportion of this excess energy will be diverted from an attractive force to one of repulsion. Upon reaching the velocity of light - relative to the prevailing gravitational field - the two opposing forces will have achieved a state of balance which would reject positively any further attempt to induce acceleration.

Seemingly, one other notable feature of rapid motion is the curious effect of time retardation - a phenomenon which is believed to have received a measure of verification through laboratory experiment, even if the mechanics involved have been far from understood. It has been found, for example, that the time required for certain unstable atomic constituents to undergo spontaneous disintegration is invariably a factor of their velocity. Although having little influence at relatively low speeds, as the velocity of light is approached this retardation effect becomes quite pronounced. Since it is logical to deduce that the disruption of such unstable particles may be attributed to a state of incompatibility existing among its constituent members, it may be wondered how an internal problem could be affected by external motion. What happens, of course, is that a higher velocity leads to the acquisition of mass in the form of a more substantial halo - an encircling swarm of minute quanta which serves to insulate the nuclear body from the outside world. But since insulation constitutes an intervening medium which works in both directions, it follows that there will exist a tendency to retain or preserve that which resides within the halo, just as surely as the same halo will act to shield if from the impacts of foreign quanta! In order for disrupted components to effect a departure they must first break through the enveloping atmosphere of the halo - a feat which takes time, and which will become somewhat more difficult should the strength of the halo be enhanced due to increased motion through a gravitational field.

Upon a philosophical basis it may now be concluded that the velocity of light represents a typical expulsion from an undeserved level of fusion, or spiritual association - *motion which is relative to the structure or entity it has just left!* Not only is the speed of radiation determined by the velocity of gravitational communion, but even the propagation of this influence is seen to be a direct reflection of a more subtle factor at work. For it would appear that one basic and universal constant of nature is the speed whereby undeserved quanta are ejected from the vicinity of material particles. In effect, the "escape velocity" imparted to expelled quanta is an expression of *unworthiness,* of total separation with respect to the system with which it was momentarily and so unjustly associated. Applied to the propagation of energy through space this means that *whatever field of influence a tiny bundle of radiation may enter, so it will be caused to travel with the velocity of light relative to that gravitational system!*

It becomes possible, at this point, to gain much needed insight into a mystery which was raised by the classical experiment pioneered by Michelson and Morley toward the close of the 19th century. Up until this time it was firmly believed that the propagation of light would obey the same fundamental laws of motion as characterize the material bodies with which we are so familiar. For instance, if we expel a projectile from a moving object - in the direction of its motion - it will inherit this initial velocity in addition to the latest thrust. This phenomenon is known as the "law of addition of speeds." It was therefore expected that light quanta, emitted from moving sources and striking other moving objects, would display variations in velocity commensurate with

THE ETERNAL UNIVERSE

such movement.

The results of experiment, however, were most conclusive and left no doubt as to the fact that something very strange must transpire with respect to tiny photons moving with extreme velocity. It was found that radiation is propagated at what appears to be a "constant" velocity; for regardless of the motions of either source or receiver the speed of impact was the same! In effect, it was as though some intangible force had intervened and accelerated any photons approaching with less than a certain speed, and resisted or slowed the motion of those approaching in excess of this same limiting velocity. The nature of this mysterious intervention may now be defined, of course, in terms of absorption and emission of energy by radiation passing through the swarms of infinitesimal quanta so permeating space and constituting a gravitational field - *essentially, a process which assures propagation at the velocity of light relative to the prevailing influence!*

Unfortunately, the Michelson-Morley experiment received a rather curious interpretation which has never been seriously questioned by any alternate theory. It has actually been assumed that when a light photon is emitted in our direction, from a receding celestial object, it will at once begin to approach our system with an effective speed of some 186,000 miles per second - while yet exhibiting an identical velocity of recession with regard to the object which it has just left! Accordingly, the distance of a receding source, in light years, is also thought to be a measure of the time (in years) that has elapsed since this light quantum first began its journey. But this view involves unwarranted and even contradictory postulates. Not only does it necessitate an unexplained break with the firmly established law whereby original motion is imparted to an ejected particle, but it further implies that when once ejected a quantum of radiation will somehow be blessed with the magical property of being able to approach, quite simultaneously, all bodies situated in its line of flight with a speed of 186,000 miles per second - irrespective of whether such bodies are approaching or receding, and provided only that the relative motion of source and final destination does not exceed the speed of light!

This entire interpretation is surely a grave mistake and, in many respects, a most obscure and impossible concept. Far from ignoring relative movement between source and receiver it may well be inferred that, subject to comparatively insignificant time lapses as multiple minor adjustments of motion are quickly effected, *radiation is propagated through the depths of space with a speed commensurate with the dictates of an expanding universe, and in full compliance with the velocities by which such bodies are approaching or receding from each other!* For all practical purposes, radiation is subject to precisely the same basic "law of addition of speeds" as material particles in general!

In effect, without realizing the full implications of traditional redshift adjustments, astronomers have been using a calculation which actually takes into consideration the perfectly valid "law of addition of speeds" - a law which was supposedly discarded with acceptance of the theory of relativity!* Ironically, in the process of translating extreme redshifts to more reasonable values (see *The Expanding Universe* section, Chapter 1), they have inadvertently stumbled upon the very formula which is capable of describing the *time* of light propagation from distant receding sources. Instead of merely a means of defining a degree of spectral displacement, the adopted Z term is really a measure of the *time required for radiation to travel from source to detection within the confines of a finite expanding universe!* (See illustration, Fig. #4.)

All that is necessary to transform a Z redshift into the true time of light propagation is to multiply it by the radius of the so-called "observable universe," expressed in light years - a figure which will always be some 1 1/2 times that of Hubble's constant! The reason for this, of course, is due to the fact that velocity (relative to the center of the universe) is steadily accelerating with distance. For example, at a point equidistant from the center and edge of a universe with an 18 BLY radius, a source would be receding at 50% of the speed of light. In order to double both velocity and distance, in one cycle of Hubble's constant, it is necessary to travel a further 9BLY and arrive at the edge of the universe with a speed equal to that of light. Since the average motion of such recession will be 75% of the velocity of light, it may be calculated

---

* It is really little short of incredible that the well established "law of addition of speeds" should be ignored when computing the time of light transit. Failure to admit that radiation could have its speed altered by some (even if yet undefined) influence, as it propagates the enormous distances between clusters of galaxies, is virtually tantamount to assuming that science is already fully versed in *all of nature's laws* - an extremely rash and unfounded assumption, to say the least!

that the time required will be of the order of 12 billion years. Hence, Hubble's constant will be 12 billion years in a universe having a radius of 18BLY. (See diagram, Fig. #5.)

In actuality the time of light transit, from many distant receding sources, will be enhanced somewhat by a rather unique and hitherto unsuspected curvature of space. Due to expansion of the universe and the steady outflowing of all matter forms - including the infinitesimal quanta so efficient in interacting with radiation - there must prevail a perpetual influence tending to push radiation toward the nearest edge of the universe. The end result, of this outward streaming of space, will be the bending of radiation received from all directions not in harmony with this overall flow. In effect, *there will appear to be a general deflection of images toward the center of the universe* - a displacement which must include all extragalactic sources not in our line of sight with either the central core or the closest boundary of the universe!

The degree of this *aberration* (or bending of the path of radiation), from remote sources partaking in the expansion of the universe, will hinge upon three factors. First, it is an effect *which is enhanced by increased distance.* Secondly, while incapable of imposing "arcing" upon radiation pursuing trajectories in harmony with the mass outward flowing of space, *it will be most pronounced at right angles to this overall movement.* (See Fig. #5.) Finally, such bending of radiation is strongly regulated by its *proximity to the edge of the universe* - in the sense that extreme curvature must arise close to the cosmic edge, where the velocity of recession approaches the speed of light itself.

THE ETERNAL UNIVERSE

Chapter 4

COSMOLOGICAL THEORIES

(Big Bang Versus Steady-state Cosmology - The Construction of Matter - Cosmic Expansion and Energy Conservation.)

With the advent of modern science a variety of cosmological theories have been proposed in an attempt to explain the origin of our physical universe. We now see that such research has been flawed by incomplete and erroneous views of gravitation and light propagation. In turn, this has led to gross misconceptions and "blind alley" models which future generations of scientists may well regard with disdain. It would not be the first instance in which a little knowledge has served to provide the fuel for wild speculation; nor is it likely to be the last, as imagination is often the key to unlocking new horizons. What does invite criticism, however, is the blatant attitude of those esteemed professionals who refuse to consider alternate ideas and the possibility of past error!

Big Bang Versus Steady-state Cosmology

Traditionally, the most widely accepted explanation for the origin of the universe has been one known as the *Big Bang* cosmology. Inspired by the realization that clusters of exterior systems are all rushing away from each other, it was perhaps inevitable that theory should picture the cosmos as arising from a gigantic explosion. Moving outward from a common center, it was first assumed that all of the elements were formed within the primordial fireball shortly after the momentous event of creation. This hypothesis was soon modified to exclude the formation of atoms heavier than hydrogen and helium, when it was realized that these elements are produced within the interiors of stars. (Also playing a role in this revision was a technical difficulty involving the build-up of complex nuclei under the prescribed conditions.) According to this concept the impetus of an explosion, which is thought to have occurred between 12 to 18 billion years ago, became translated into an expanding universe as clouds of hydrogen atoms condensed locally into individual galaxies and stars.

Certain philosophical implications are inherent in the nature of this view. First and foremost, it implies that the universe was created at one specific moment in the past. Hence, at some time in the future, it will have aged to the stage where it is no longer able to support biological life. Upon this premise clusters of galaxies will simply continue to recede from each other until, finally, the sky will be void of all exterior systems beyond one's own gravitationally bound cluster. This model is finite in both time and physical constitution. An obvious issue which arises involves the purpose of creation. What motivation lies behind the origin of matter, and of the subsequent life forms which it nurtures? On the basis of this concept the universe appears highly transitory in essence. Moreover, if God be the Creator, where was He before? Did He also come into existence at the same time as the universe? More questions are surely raised than are answered.

From a purely scientific standpoint this model is beset by serious inconsistencies involving the time factor. In brief, the ages of some celestial objects do not appear compatible with the supposition that the universe was created at one particular instant in the past. While certain portions are unquestionably very old, other regions give every indication of comparatively recent formation. Indeed, even a cursory examination of quasars is sufficient to reveal a contradiction. For instance, since it is generally agreed that the life expectancy of a quasar is much less than the implied age of the universe, one cannot avoid wondering why some nearby quasars are still shining brightly as such if they were all formed about the same time as others whose light would reveal them to be in existence more than a dozen billion years ago!

Building upon advantages inherent in an explosive origin, a modified oscillating version of the Big Bang was soon developed and came to be favored by many cosmologists. This concept visualizes the recession of the galaxies as being slowed by gravitation. Upon this premise it is inferred that expansion will ultimately be converted to contraction, so that all matter may be brought together with such force as to produce periodic explosions upon a truly cosmic scale. In effect, the universe would be seen to oscillate between states of expansion and contraction. Although appearing to eliminate the problem of initial origin, there has been much debate as to whether or not sufficient mass exists (even upon the basis of traditional views of gravitation) with which to produce a closed universe. But a crucial objection to this model is posed by the thought of radiation escaping from the outer extremities of such a universe; for there is simply no way for lost energy to be recovered! To appeal to gravitation is not only useless, but would imply that the weakest field could exert a drastic influence upon the motion of radiation - in itself, a supposition directly opposed to traditional views of light propagation! Should just one quantum escape, with each cycle of expansion and contraction, in time an oscillating universe would be literally dissipated into space. Accordingly, the concept has all the aspects of a monstrous contradiction!

An interesting alternative, known as the *Steady-state* or *Continuous Creation* principle, was proposed around the middle of the 20th century. This model holds that the universe is infinite in time, in the sense that as matter is lost through the process of cosmic expansion it is replaced by the creation of an equivalence of new matter - in the voids between the clusters of galaxies - so that the overall structure of the universe is retained. Inability to account for the powerful driving force behind the expansion of the universe, long considered to be an exceedingly weak feature of this concept, is now seen to pose no problem upon the basis of our new views of gravitational repulsion!

Shortly after the Continuous Creation principle was given serious consideration observational data began to raise strong doubts as to its validity. The detection of a curious microwave radiation background was thought, by many astronomers, to be far more consistent with the Big Bang principle. Subsequently, this radio noise has been interpreted as the fading remnant of an intense primordial fireball announcing the birth of our universe. During the 1960's yet another blow to the Steady-state view was delivered by the radio telescope. It was found that the number of peculiar radio sources was greater than what might be expected from a simple increase of volume with distance. Many of these sources are believed to represent galaxies (and quasars) at a rather short-lived and eventful stage of evolution - presumably, one tending to be more frequent with youth. Since, in looking out into space one is also going back into time, it was inferred that (upon the basis of a superdense origin) man should be able to see the more distant portions of the universe when these objects were younger and less scattered through expansion - in apparent

THE ETERNAL UNIVERSE

agreement with observation.

Now the astonishing conclusion to emerge is that scientific evidence, as currently interpreted, stands in flat contradiction to all of these cosmological models in some crucial respect! We know that this cannot be so, since one of the two basic creation choices must be essentially correct. Nevertheless, this is exactly the prevailing state of confusion and frustration posed by the study of radiation from distant sources - information enabling man to probe billions of years into the past. The present overwhelming preference of astronomers for the Big Bang principle is due, not so much to the absence of criticism, as it is to seemingly insurmountable objections to the alternate Continuous Creation cosmology!

As a result of this curious impasse, which is reached when one attempts to determine the true cosmological model, it is well to ask whether our dilemma might not arise because of an erroneous assumption with regard to the manner in which radiation is propagated within an expanding universe. Indeed, it is surely more than a mere coincidence that, in almost every instance, the *time* element is somehow directly involved in a damaging contradiction of the various cosmological models!

It turns out that the one outstanding feature to be noted from our study of radiation propagation is that the redshifts, detected in the light received from distant receding systems, contains a hitherto unrecognized factor. Such Doppler shift measurements must reflect not only genuine velocity of recession, but also the distance - expressed in terms of an apparent increase of velocity - by which the universe has expanded during the time that elapses while radiation travels from source to detection! In short, the redshift in the light of a receding system is really a composite of velocity of recession and cosmic expansion - *essentially, a measure of the time that radiation has spent in transit!*

While it may be a valid premise to state that the velocity of light is a constant relative to the prevailing gravitational field, *it will be understood that such fields are themselves in motion as they share in the expansion of the universe!* Necessitating a reinstatement of the "law of addition of speeds," the cosmological implications of this revised concept of radiation propagation are truly enormous - plainly bespeaking the uncritical acceptance of a false assumption residing at the very roots of contemporary science! Invariably, it holds the key to a solution of the creation impasse.

THE ETERNAL UNIVERSE

Of foremost concern is the realization that any attempt to deduce the age and origin of the universe from its rate of expansion is fraught with an unsuspected hazard. It has been the custom of astronomers to accept the distance of a remote galaxy (in light years) as synonymous with the number of years required by light to make this journey. We now see that this view must be incorrect and could readily lead to a gross underestimation of the time involved, since light emitted from a receding galaxy is able to approach our system with an effective speed of 186,000 miles per second only after it has actually entered our own gravitational field. *By far the greatest proportion of its journey is characterized by a velocity of approach that is somewhat less than this speed!* Hence, there will be a discrepancy in time of light propagation, as implied by orthodox and revised concepts - a difference that is almost negligible for neighboring clusters of galaxies, but which assumes overwhelming importance when the more remote clusters are considered. (See Fig. #4.)

By virtue of this revised view of radiation propagation it becomes possible to refute evidence which many astronomers have come to accept as conclusive in eliminating the Steady-state cosmology as a viable model. Hitherto, the discovery of an excessive number of comparatively short-lived extragalactic radio sources (beyond what might be expected from a simple increase of space/volume with distance) seemed inexplicable in terms of the Steady-state principle. Needless to say, this observation has been interpreted as proof of a superdense origin, since it is inferred that this increase must mean that such objects were much closer together in the remote past.

But once more we would be guilty of jumping to a false conclusion. Instead of our telescopes (both radio and optical) probing equally into space and time, it must follow that - at high redshifts - more powerful instruments are actually overcoming *far more time than distance,* due to expansion of the universe and the increased time needed by radiation to catch up to rapidly moving systems! (It is, of course, quite immaterial whether it is the emitting or receiving body which is doing the moving - the overall effect being the same.) However, if the Steady-state view is valid this also means that we are observing an enhanced proportion of galaxies and quasars which were in their youth at some time in the very distant past. The mounting incidence of radio sources with distance is therefore not surprising; for as one goes back into time

THE ETERNAL UNIVERSE

- at an ever greater rate than distance - so more objects will be made to reveal characteristics typical of all stages of cosmic evolution! Rather than detecting larger numbers of remote sources in a smaller volume of space, it will be acknowledged that more objects of a significant age group have simply been observed. *In effect, we are able to view substantially more than one generation of creation!*

What were once considered impressive objections to the Steady-state principle are thus revealed to be without foundation. But the workings of prejudice are not readily overcome. An entire generation of astronomers and physicists has been taught to accept - without question - the idea of a Big Bang cosmology. It will not be easy for many scientists to admit that they have dismissed an alternate theory which should have been given every consideration. It becomes even more difficult when it is realized that this decision was based upon an obviously flawed fundamental scientific precept! Although it is almost inconceivable that present views of radiation propagation ever came to be established, this digression must be dealt with in the manner of genuine science - namely, through honest and impartial analysis of all available evidence. In so doing, a truly amazing picture of the cosmos will be seen to unfold.

Should we accept the proposed revision of radiation propagation, which implies that we have already detected objects with light transit times some tens of billions of years greater than what is permissible upon the basis of any explosive origin of the universe, *then there is no alternative but to conclude that the principle of Continuous Creation emerges in sole agreement with the evidence!*

Nevertheless, it is also evident that the Steady-state cosmology, as presently understood, is very much in need of certain elaboration and modification. In particular, it must be clear that the introduction of elementary matter forms cannot possibly occur at the level of the hydrogen atom, which is now seen to represent a highly evolved state from the initial creation of a lowly infinitesimal quantum, or "A". Also requiring clarification is the microwave background radiation, which is thought to argue in favor of an explosion from a superdense singularity. Similarly, many fundamental problems relating to the unique physical properties of matter remain unanswered.

THE ETERNAL UNIVERSE

The Construction of Matter

Without a doubt, a most pressing unsolved characteristic of matter is that of electricity, a strange influence which may be expressed as a force of either attraction or repulsion. While a force of exceedingly short range it is also an extremely powerful phenomenon, completely dominating the nature of matter at close distances. But just what is electricity? Why do two "positive" or two "negative" charges repel each other; and why do two unlike charges attract?

A possible explanation suggests itself. Recalling the basic premise that an inborn desire for fusion will serve to induce a cloud of infinitesimal quanta to congregate about a material particle, it may well prove advantageous to ask if *halo rotation* might not somehow be at the root of this highly concentrated force. What, in fact, would be the consequences of postulating the existence of a cosmic law which recognizes but two fundamental and opposed states of particle rotation? May we not assume that "A" is created of opposite "charges" - essentially, specific directions of rotation? Most assuredly, this assumption would be in full accord with the universal principle which states: "For every action there is an equal and opposite reaction."

Two crucial difficulties must be overcome before this view will merit serious consideration, the first of which concerns the implied limitation of rotation to but two opposed directions. How is it possible for an electrically charged particle to always display one specific charge (or direction of rotation) relative to other charged bodies - especially since it may approach them at any one of an innumerable number of angles?

Actually, this problem is not nearly so formidable as it might appear, and probably arises solely because we are inclined to visualize rotation as something which transpires in but one direction at a time. But singular motion is capable of expressing only a flat two-dimensional universe, whereas it is clear that we live in a world consisting of three basic geometric dimensions. The difficulty is at once resolved if, in addition to an equatorial rotation, we also postulate a simultaneous polar rotation. In other words, whatever polar and equatorial rotations may characterize a particle of negative charge, so a positive charge is to be interpreted as the flow or movement of energy in precisely the opposite rotary directions. Upon this premise it will follow that two unlike electrical charges will always exhibit properties consistent with their relative flows of energy, quite regardless of the angle of approach! Similarly, two like charges will also be unaffected by the direction of approach and will express themselves in a manner peculiar to such relative motions.

This entire effect, incidentally, may be demonstrated rather convincingly by bringing together two spherical objects, and by imparting the appropriate rotations in order to simulate a variety of like and unlike charges. It will be found that, no matter what angle the two spherical bodies of *like rotation* are caused to come into mutual contact, *the motions of their respective surfaces will oppose or clash!* Conversely, the two bodies of *unlike rotation* will always *flow in harmony with each other at the point where they touch!* This principle of opposed flows is surely of great significance to an understanding of the mechanics of electrical interaction. (The various types of particle spin theorized by physicists, in an attempt to explain certain phenomena, may well be reconciled with such a concept on the grounds that they merely constitute *secondary* motions superimposed upon a much faster and more basic trait.)

The second major difficulty involves an explanation of the observed state of repulsion and attraction among the two forms of electricity. Fortunately, the answer to this first problem provides us with a promising clue. Noting that similar rotary motions always clash head-on when brought together, whereas unlike rotary flows will merge and share a common motion at the point where contact is made, it is not difficult to connect such occurrences with the effects of repulsion and attraction, respectively.

When two particles of like charge approach within a critical distance of each other their swirling halos will collide, with the result that a substantial proportion of their total energy content will be transformed into "neutral quanta" at the point of impact. Unless the nuclei of the two particles come together with sufficient force to burst through the encircling atmospheres of their mutual halos - thereby accomplishing an act of fusion - this new concentration of energy must be released with explosive violence following a very brief period of compression. In essence, the repulsion of two particles of like charge may be attributed to a sudden exposure to more energy than can be "processed" (e.g., absorbed and emitted) without posing a critical injustice to the involved nuclear bodies - in the sense that such spiritual entities will be intimately associated with far more "A" than they deserve! In this event the magnitude of the injustice will prevent a strong influx of "neutral quanta" from lingering long enough to be whirled around the body of a major particle and ejected in the opposite direction from whence received. Instead, this excess energy will be promptly rejected and expelled in much the same direction from which it arrived, thus imparting a thrust away from the vicinity of the impact site.

In direct contrast to this explosive state we may examine instances of two unlike charges coming into close association. Since the two flows of energy are essentially compatible, at the instant of contact, the production of "neutral quanta" - through halo collision - will not immediately exceed the ability of the two approaching bodies to "process" this energy. What now transpires is really tantamount to raising the question of what prevents an unlimited contraction of a positive-negative pair. Initially, the mutual penetration of halos must serve to produce only a modest increase of "neutral quanta," with an appropriate acceleration in velocity of approach beyond that which could be expected from gravitation alone. With the incidence of collision among halo quanta increasing as penetration progresses, the two rotary flows of energy will intersect at angles which tend more and more to oppose each other. As a result, a rising proportion of this "fuel" will be encountered in such a manner as to induce a spiraling motion - specifically, a thrust imparted at somewhat of an angle to a line which would characterize a direct approach. Following a brief period of intense acceleration, as this increased supply of "fuel" is put to use, the stage will be reached when orbital velocity becomes sufficient to offset any attractive force. At this point a balance will be established and the pair will enter into a stable orbit, rotating about a common center and separated by a distance commensurate with the total mass of the system.

It would therefore appear that we are justified in upholding the principle of opposed motion as a key to an understanding of this basic trait of matter - a characteristic presumably initiated with the creation of "A" and perpetuated through the evolution of infinitesimal quanta to such ultimate particles as the electron and proton. Upon a philosophical plane one might choose to interpret this electrical aspect of creation as a divided state somewhat analogous to our own sex-divided world - whereby an incentive exists for all "unbalanced" members to seek mutual balance and progress through union with oppositely "unbalanced" entities.

We may well come to the conclusion that the mysterious phenomenon of electricity is but a unique manifestation of gravitation. In all probability, this force is simply a *highly condensed rotary flow of gravitational energy* - perhaps little wonder that our past failure to explain the nature of this communion should also coincide with the inability to define electricity!

As an approach to the actual construction of matter - from its inception as lowly "A" - a number of relevant mysteries may be cited. What, for example, determines the sizes or masses of the various atomic particles? How, in fact, are they even formed at all? If radiation represents a variety of particles intermediate in size between an "A" and the level of an electron, then why are such structures unable to engage in evolutionary matter-building activities? Why are there no anti-protons outside of extremely short-lived laboratory freaks? Why are free electrons so much more plentiful than their opposite counterpart, the positron, which is practically an unknown commodity as a free entity in our section of the universe? How can the properties of neutral particles be explained? Why are neutrons so unstable outside of an atomic nucleus? Further, how do they accomplish the feat of binding together protons which would otherwise repel each other?

Proceeding upon the basis that the Steady-state model is indeed the selected method of introducing creation, we may now face the problem of describing the evolution of matter from the lowly status of an "A".

It is clear, first of all, that new creation cannot occur at random throughout the expanse of the universe. Most assuredly, it is likely to take place in response to a significant *absence of matter* - a vacuum of such exacting proportions as to be found only between the clusters of galaxies themselves! Thus we may visualize creation as a phenomenon transpiring in the voids between all clusters of galaxies, and proceeding at just the required rate to replace that matter which is lost through expansion of the universe. As a result, new creation zones will develop and be centered between existing aggregations of matter as soon as density and gravitational influence reaches a critical minimum - from whence creation will appear to spread out and assume the form of expanding shells as it follows the recession of surrounding clusters of galaxies.

But if the introduction of newly created "A" is confined to regions of extreme vacuum, how are elementary forms able to condense, in the time permitted, to a degree sufficient to produce such highly compacted structures as electrons and protons? Obviously, at some crucial stage, a sparse distribution of "A" must be transformed into regions of great density - from whence the fusion process is enabled to function with vastly increased efficiency. The problem is thus seen to be one of transporting widely scattered quanta to a common meeting point.

Inasmuch as gravitational attraction cannot be evoked during the earlier stages of condensation, we are left with the *repulsive* aspect of gravity and radiation as a viable alternative. Converging from all directions in space toward the center of an expanding creation zone, between neighboring superclusters of galaxies, this steady streaming of energy facilitates a chain reaction effect. That is to say, once a collision has occurred between a photon (or exceptionally massive quantum) and a recently created infinitesimal "A", both entities will proceed to further encounters, etc. In time, the result must be a veritable deluge of elementary matter forms flowing toward a central point of sufficient density as to ensure fusion into such fundamental structures as electrons, positrons and protons. Since the energy required to condense "A" is equal to that needed to push an equivalence of mass apart, it is tantamount to yet another demonstration of Newton's Third Law of Motion: "To every action there is always an equal and contrary reaction." Essentially the exchange of extragalactic energy accomplishes a twofold purpose, *as the condensation of "A" is seen to be achieved at the expense of producing an expanding universe!*

The next major problem to confront us concerns the question of particle size. For while it is obvious that a direct fusion of larger and larger quantities of elementary matter forms cannot continue indefinitely, it very much remains to be explained how nature has contrived to impose the observed limitations in the sizes of such stable and "maximum" particles as electrons and positrons, and the somewhat higher level of the proton.

According to a well established scientific law the rotation of a spinning body will be enhanced with either a reduction of diameter (assuming that there is no loss of mass) or an increase in mass leading to a rise in density. Inasmuch as the fusion of greater quantities of energy or matter into one larger mass is in full agreement with this last requirement, it could well follow that the solution to the problem of particle size is to be found therein. For the very act of increasing rotation - through the incorporation of additional mass - must produce more violent collisions with newly encountered quanta. Should the force of these impacts exceed a critical value this excess quanta will be accelerated to escape velocity in an extremely short span of time. Furthermore, as rotation approaches the speed of light, so the efficiency of gravitational communion will be greatly reduced - *becoming non-existent once this limiting velocity is attained!* Essentially, the evolution of a "maximum" material particle is seen to be a self-terminating process.

The fusion of elementary quanta into a "maximum" particle is thus very much linked to the issue of gravitational communion. Take, for instance, the case of a partially evolved structure encountering additional quanta. In order to incorporate this energy it is vital that relative velocities be such as to allow *intimate association for a minimum interval of time!* Time must be given for a critical degree of communion to be established, including a possible exchange of the spiritual entities so involved. We can now readily see why radiation is unable to evolve to higher material structures. For while we cannot appeal to the hypothesis of a "maximum" particle with a critical velocity of rotation to account for the unsociable characteristics of radiation, we can explain this reluctance to undergo evolutionary fusion on the grounds of insufficient time. Due to its extreme motion through space it is virtually impossible for radiation to establish the required association with foreign quanta - a requirement demanding intimate communion and close proximity of components for a minimum length of time!

On the whole, it will be inferred that the evolution of material structures may proceed in a more or less straightforward manner until the electron-positron level is reached, at which point rotation has grown sufficient to forbid a direct addition of further quanta. Henceforth, evolution may continue only through associations of entire electrons and positrons - a new and comparatively brief round of matter-building which eventually terminates in the construction of the proton. Since, for a presumably similar reason, a proton also represents a "maximum" particle, it follows that continued evolution must embrace a fusion of masses of the general order of protons - a process which is even more restrictive and soon terminates at the level of the heavier elements. Complicated somewhat by a constant struggle of proton-neutron complexes to preserve unity, excessive mass may again jeopardize stability by allowing motion to become a regulating factor.

As contraction of the primordial clouds progresses in regions between superclusters of galaxies, so elementary forms of matter will continue to grow with the fusion of more and more quanta of a compatible nature. With the passage of time swarms of "A" of opposite charge will come together in roughly equal proportion, and in such manner as to preserve the initial state of but two opposed directions of rotation. That is to say, while a degree of random orbital motion may be described immediately following an occasion of fusion, it is bound to be of a very temporary nature and the components will soon be induced to adopt an overall momentum in harmony with one of the two inherent rotary directions. Were some arbitrary motion substituted the surfaces of the initial pair of quanta would clash and generate a repulsive force which would tend to shift this orbital plane until a harmonious relationship is established - namely, an association in accord with the proposition that the resulting charge will be the one requiring the least adjustment in order to adopt one of the two permitted rotary motions. Similarly, should some relatively small quantum seek incorporation into an evolving particle it will be compelled to share this same general rotation, as no component could escape collision were it to continue to orbit contrary to the prevailing flow of energy.

Although the formation of equal quantities of positrons and electrons may be deduced from theory the evolution of protons, without accompanying anti-protons, remains a vital issue to be clarified. Clearly, we are confronted with a drastic departure from established procedure - a point which strongly suggests the introduction of some subtle influence at a crucial stage in the contraction of a primordial cloud. In this respect there would appear to exist only one phenomenon to which we might appeal: the overall rotation characterizing a cloud of elementary matter forms!

But this assumption promptly raises the question of how contracting clouds could always manage to acquire one specific direction of rotation. At the risk of seeming to evade an issue, by deferring a possible answer, it may nevertheless prove advantageous to pursue the premise that rotation of a primordial cloud -

in the same direction as that of a proton - is the key to the construction of protons without an opposite counterpart. Perhaps, in so doing, a solution to this mystery will present itself.

Given a modest incentive to engage in a rotary movement at some appropriate phase prior to its climax, and considering the vast distance over which condensation must occur, it may be deduced that tremendous rotational velocity will develop toward the latter stages of a cloud's contraction. Of particular significance is the fact that rotation will vary greatly with the distance from the center; that is, the more central regions will revolve at speeds much faster than the outlying portions. With this thought in mind we may contemplate the union of positrons and electrons as they stream toward the center of a primordial cloud.

As newly constructed electrons and positrons enter the dense and rapidly rotating nuclear region of the cloud they will be observed to approach from a direction somewhat *perpendicular to the prevailing flow of energy!* Spiraling deeper into the core of the swirling cloud, a discrimination will soon arise with regard to the direction in which fusion is most liable to be facilitated. In effect, there will be a mounting preference for recent arrivals to be incorporated at the *leading edges* of developing positron-electron complexes. Not only must it follow that an evolving structure will encounter more potential members in the direction of its motion, but it will also be more difficult for particles to enter into a relationship from the opposite direction and with the principal body tending to move away at high speed.

As a direct consequence of this discrimination a strong incentive will eventually prevail for an evolving complex to adopt a rotation in harmony with that of the cloud itself. A little reflection is sufficient to show that violent collisions - hence repulsion - will ensue at the leading edge of an evolving structure unless it shares the basic rotary motion of the primordial cloud! Only if compatible rotation is present will the surface of a developing particle flow in harmony with the momentum expressed by the majority of encountered forms. Confronted with an adverse flow of energy, most positron-electron unions which do occur in the reverse direction will tend to be disrupted before the final stages of proton construction are reached - with any survivors being annihilated through later encounters with overwhelming numbers of protons.

Now it is obvious that the contraction of a primordial cloud, with a steady acceleration in velocity of rotation, cannot continue indefinitely. For while an appreciable density is required at some stage of creation in order to expedite the evolution of material particles, the observed distribution of matter within the universe makes it fully apparent that this must be a very temporary state - invariably, *a state preceding a mammoth explosion!*

The mechanism triggering this cataclysm must surely involve the tremendous rotary forces which exist deep within the cloud as it reaches an advanced stage of contraction, and shortly following a large-scale production of protons. As the innermost regions are accelerated to velocities approaching the limiting speed of light, so a strong braking action will arise as material particles begin to resist further acceleration. Intense pressure will build up, in a manner somewhat analogous to that of a powerful coil spring being wound to maximum tension. Although a supermassive black hole is readily formed at the center of a contracting primordial cloud, it is prevented from swallowing up all condensing matter forms by reason of extreme rotational velocity which greatly reduces the efficiency of gravitational attraction. (In conformity with the curve of Fig. #2, the effectiveness of gravitation may be visualized as becoming non-existent at the velocity of light.) As a result, the inherent nature of protons to repel each other leads to increased motion and even less susceptibility to gravitational containment. Since heat may best be described as "motion of impact," it is clear that truly astronomical temperatures will ultimately be reached in the vicinity of the core. In fact, were it not for the overwhelming force of material still streaming inward, the nucleus of the cloud would be induced to shatter at a relatively early stage. Compressed by the sheer weight of inflowing matter, the core must continue to grow hotter and rotate with ever greater rapidity. For some time this rising outward pressure may thus be contained until, at last, the core is caused to explode with a violence sufficient to blast the vast bulk of all matter forms into the depths of space - *from whence the ejected particles will later condense into what is essentially a supercluster of galaxies!*

Although on a scale which far surpases that of a mere supernova eruption, widely differing circumstances will conspire to mask any outward signs of such a stupendous event. The exceedingly powerful gravitational field, combined with innumerable encounters that are highly conducive to fusion due to favorable relative motion, must facilitate the incorporation of all but an infinitesimal fragment of the cloud's total mass-energy into "maximum" particles. With gravity tending to prevent expelled radiation from fully achieving escape velocity, along with the presence of huge swarms of only partially evolved structures, it will be seen that an exceptionally strong incentive exists for free quanta to be promptly absorbed by these undeveloped material forms.

Vestiges of this dynamic matter-building process - implying successive generations of *Small Bang* explosions - are very likely to be found in the peculiar nature of *quasars!* Since it is most logical to suspect that remnants of these superdense sites will persist, in one form or another, it is well to consider related features. The combination of extreme density and substantial mass, which is believed to constitute a unique characteristic of quasars, is in precise agreement with what might be inferred of a nuclear core left over from a superdense explosion. Indeed, the presence of a supermassive black hole, at the center of a quasar, is exactly what would be anticipated under the prescribed conditions! (With the core of a collapsing primordial cloud severely elongated through extreme centrifugal force, the ensuing explosion could very well act to spew the bulk of matter in opposite directions. Accordingly, it may be predicted that - with the passage of time - dual superclusters of galaxies could tend to evolve out of individual Small Bangs. In turn, this leads to the possibility of our being able to deduce the relative ages of such concentrations from their separations.)

Of all the "maximum" particles, so formed within a Small Bang creation site, it is the positron that is most suited to achieve a total escape into regions of future creation zones - providing subsequent generations with the necessary rotary impetus for the formation of protons. The reason why free positrons are unique in their ability to escape is due to a most favorable mass to velocity ratio. While possessing sufficient size and momentum to overcome resistance through impacts with surrounding quanta, they are also small enough to be accelerated to escape velocity. Protons, on the other hand, cannot be imparted with the same velocity and must be contained by gravitation to form galaxies of stars. Attracted to protons by virtue of compatible electric charge, almost all free electrons may be expected to be trapped into association. With this acquisition of an encircling electron a proton is transformed into an atom of hydrogen, the principal source of stellar fuel and a fundamental building block of our physical universe. (The production of primordial helium, beyond what may be accounted for by stellar burning of hydrogen, is now seen to have a ready explanation in the concept of Small Bangs.)

Not only are we thus enabled to explain the absence of free positrons in our sector of space, but this inferred large-scale ejection of positive charges into regions between the superclusters provides a clue to the solution of another mystery - namely, the deferred issue as to how the primordial clouds could always be induced to adopt the specific rotary direction of a proton. In effect, a positron enriched nucleus will incite elementary forms to partake of this same general motion as they arrive in the more central regions of the swirling cloud. Influenced by the presence of a predominant number of positive charges, the cores of all primordial clouds may be expected to acquire this common rotary trait at a crucial stage of condensation - from whence it is bound to be perpetuated through successive generations of creation!

The formation of neutrons may be looked upon as a process occurring in the intense heat and density of stellar interiors. When a pair of protons are brought together with sufficient force to achieve a mutual penetration of halos, the two nuclei will remain in close association within the confines of a reconstituted overall halo which quickly assumes a characteristic proton rotation. By inferring the presence of an electron nucleus (an electron largely stripped of its halo), the stability of such a union may well be explicable in terms of two positive charges exchanging a negative charge. Thus, at any given moment, one of the proton nuclei will have temporary custody of the electron nucleus and may, in a sense, be considered to be the neutron.

The normal tendency of two protons to repel each other will be negated once all threat of violent halo collisions is removed, and when the compatible rotary motion of an electron nucleus is permitted to intercede and act as a "lubricant" between the surfaces of two proton nuclei that would otherwise clash and generate intense friction. Assuming that only a modest amount of the most minute quanta is retained within an atomic nucleus as localized halos of minor value, energy may be exchanged by the nuclear components in such a way as to produce a favorable supply of useable "neutral quanta." With gravitational/electrical attraction thus enhanced to an enormous degree, a short-range binding force of considerable strength may be postulated. Yet another feature contributing to internal stability is that of the overall halo itself - an energy barrier which must impose the same restraint upon escape as it does with regard to any inward penetration.

How are we to account for this seemingly fortuitous appearance of an electron nucleus? In all probability it is simply *created* at the moment of nuclear fusion- presumably, out of the halo energy enveloping the protons. Indeed, as two such halos are forcibly driven together a certain amount of impacted halo quanta will be compressed between the two spinning bodies and caused to adopt a specific motion - rotary momentum determined by the angle of the intersecting energy flows which, in this instance, will be seen to be opposite that of a proton! When this swirling accumulation of energy reaches a critical mass-density it will literally result in the creation of an electron nucleus - a "maximum" particle whose evolution terminates with a rejection of further quanta.

Technically, the ability of an electron to neutralize the charge of a proton must embrace the principle of *interference,* whether it be a case of movement through an atmospheric halo or the interaction of nuclei at the center of such an enveloping cloud of energy. In the former instance the disruptive influence of an oppositely rotating electron halo will serve to cancel outward effects of rotary motion. In the case of a neutron this disturbance of the overall rotary flow is perpetrated from within. By reason of a nuclear electron's rapid orbital motion around a proton nucleus, and in conjunction with inherent tendencies to incite opposite halo rotation, the original halo structure of the proton will be so disrupted that no significant rotary flow of energy will be established. In short, a neutral particle may be defined as either a *cancellation or absence of any specific halo rotation!*

Due to the greatly reduced halos surrounding components of an atomic nucleus, a nuclear electron is probably permitted to spiral toward the actual surface of the proton nucleus - from which point the repulsive properties of a "maximum" particle will prevail and, in the process of preventing a direct incorporation of unwarranted energy, will accelerate the smaller body to a higher orbit. In brief, it will be called upon to describe an orbit of considerable eccentricity as it is periodically repelled after coming into virtual contact with a rapidly spinning proton nucleus. As a result of this highly eccentric movement, which is perhaps reminiscent of the orbit of a periodic comet, the stability of a free neutron must be somewhat in jeopardy, requiring only the impact of an especially large quantum of energy at a strategic moment to literally propel the nuclear electron clear out of the system. As a consequence of inhabiting a compound atomic nucleus, however, a wandering nuclear electron will almost invariably encounter another proton nucleus before it can manage to escape, thereby assuring the stability of the structure.

The unstable family of mesons, with masses intermediate between protons and electrons, may well be interpreted as segments of protons - bundles of electron and positron nuclei torn loose following violent collisions involving atomic nuclei. The heavier class of so-called particles known as hyperons, with masses rated in excess of the proton, are evidently larger aggregations of positron/electron nuclei remaining together for the smallest fraction of a second before dispersing from similar impact sites. During such brief intervals (often less than one ten-billionth of a second!) both positive and negative characteristics may be exhibited, along with disturbing motions which would give rise to neutral properties. Tentative associations of this sort, including freak transient quarks and gluon-type peculiarities, are made possible by the inability of a system to change its mass-energy relationship in zero time.

Even the rather elusive neutrino, a hypothetical particle of no apparent charge and virtually no mass (almost entirely energy of motion), introduced by science to balance certain equations relating to nuclear events, must now receive interpretation in terms of ejected gravitational quanta! Instead of actual material particles traveling with a variety of extreme speeds, in all probability they are simply specific - and varying - bundles of minute quanta leaving the site of some nuclear transformation with the velocity of light.

Incidently, the formation of a "maximum" particle may well have much in common with the structure of a black hole. Just as extreme rotation is believed to impose an eventual limit with regard to the incorporation of "A", so this same factor is likely to shed new insight into black holes. With the efficiency of gravitational attraction undergoing a rapid decline as velocity approaches light speed, so it must become more difficult for a singularity to induce further assimilation of mass-energy. Contrary to some popular notions of black holes, which would have them literally swallowing everything in their vicinity, extreme motion must severely limit the many course corrections needed to direct infalling matter forms toward an infinitesimal singularity. Spiraling rapidly toward such a pinpoint entity, the vast majority of ingested matter will surely escape by reason of *deflection!* Accordingly, it is little wonder that this unique property of a black hole is capable of generating the prodigious power output of a quasar! (Upon this basis the formation of a supermassive black hole is likely accomplished by the simple expedient of combining vast numbers of stellar-sized singularities.)

Cosmic Expansion and Energy Conservation

With the phenomenon of gravitation receiving interpretation as the inborn desire of all creation to fulfill its Destiny through the process of *Cosmic Fusion,* we were soon made aware of a serious misconception which had hitherto prevailed regarding the propagation of radiation. In turn, clarification of this issue served to reveal the Steady-state principle to be the foundation upon which a successful cosmology must be based. And yet, as if by way of a paradox, even the explosive origin concept was seen to have merit when modified to embrace a never-ending series of Small Bangs announcing the birth of "maximum" particles. But this unexpected blend of cosmological models raises a number of unanswered questions - not the least of which involves the problem of reconciling the "law of energy conservation" with the idea of *continuous creation* and a *finite expanding universe!* Another crucial point which demands further reflection is that of the *size* of the universe itself. Together, they hold the key to an understanding of the Great Cosmic Pyramid, and of a truly momentous prediction regarding the fate of our physical universe. (No matter how astonishing a conclusion may seem, if there is no other alternative then its validity must be upheld!)

Of itself, the very character of the Steady-state model involves a contradiction with the firmly established scientific principle known as the "conservation of energy" - whereby the total mass-energy content of the universe is viewed as an interchangeable but fixed commodity. Inasmuch as a continuous creation of new matter must imply a steady increase in the size of our physical cosmos, it is clear that stability may only be maintained through *a literal disintegration of an equivalence of existing matter!* Just as there is birth and death in the realm of biological life, so at the level of physical matter there must be a reconciliation of creation with a precisely opposite factor. Somewhere, and somehow, matter must surely be caused to sever its bonds with the empirical world and vanish just as mysteriously as it made its initial appearance! Invariably, the laws regulating this departure will be seen to be no less revealing than those governing the introduction of infinitesimal "A" between the clusters of galaxies.

Nor is there any way of evading the issue of disintegration. Strange though it might first seem there can be no question of doubt. For instance, if we were to postulate a universe infinite solely in physical dimensions we would not have a truly infinite universe! Without new creation all stars must, in time, age and die. What, then, will become of our so-called infinite universe? On the other hand, should we attempt to add a creation factor to our universe of infinite dimensions we are immediately faced with a flat contradiction. How can we possibly place an endless quantity of new matter in a universe that is already infinite in size - without achieving infinite density? Obviously, there can be but one solution. Only through the premise of a cosmos *finite* in physical dimensions can we hope to escape the dilemma of having no place to put new creation!

In order to reconcile Steady-state philosophy with the assumption that the universe is finite in size we must picture creation as a process which transpires - between clusters of galaxies - within the confines of a vast spherical region of space. Outside of this Cosmic Creation Zone no elementary matter forms may be born - *a supposition which very much suggests that matter, as such, is unable to exist in regions so unduly separated from the remainder of creation!* Indeed, since a violation of the "law of energy conservation" may only be avoided by predicting the annihilation of a specific quantity of matter, and in a specific interval of time, a disintegration factor based upon a critical separation or lack of overall communion is an inevitable conclusion. Presumably, recession of the outermost systems - *at the velocity of light* - forbids their continued association with creation as a whole. If so, *an abrupt disintegration is the fate which awaits those onrushing systems attaining this critical limit - essentially, a crucial distance and velocity of recession relative to the center of the universe!*

A deeper insight into this inferred disintegration is likely to be found upon consideration of implications inherent in our revised

THE ETERNAL UNIVERSE

concept of energy propagation. Invariably, reinstatement of the "law of addition of speeds" must raise the issue as to what really transpires at the precise edge of the universe, where radiation becomes totally trapped by the phenomenon of cosmic expansion. Without a doubt, a truly amazing situation must develop which, in certain respects, reminds one of the principle expounded by Olbers' paradox. Heinrich Olbers, a 19th century German astronomer, dared to ask the seemingly absurd question as to why the night sky appeared dark. His argument took the eventual form that the universe could not be infinite in both physical dimensions and time, since the combined light of an infinite number of distant stars would serve to make incoming radiation of the intensity of the surface of the average star! We now know, of course, that an expanding universe is capable of resolving this paradox, which is also seen to have a solution in the concept of a finite universe. Nevertheless, this same principle arises, in a somewhat different (but very drastic) form, at the extreme boundary of our physical universe.

As light-emitting galaxies of stars - along with such concentrated energy sources as supernovae and quasars - reach the edge of the universe their radiation will, in effect, become trapped to form an encircling *"shell of energy."* Since any inflowing radiation, emitted at the cosmic edge, will be receding at some 100% light speed (relative to the center of the universe), it will remain essentially *stationary - in a sense, trapped indefinitely in a universe that is infinite in time!* The sheer magnitude of this invisible shell is bound to tax the imagination, simply because of the infinity of time aspect which must allow radiation to add upon radiation. In all probability, *the inferred disintegration is accomplished through violent collision - at the edge of the universe - when material structures (e.g., stars, planets, etc.) strike this enveloping shell of intense energy at the velocity of light!*

So concentrated is this fateful energy field that it may, in fact, be likened unto an *encircling black hole!* Quite invisible to the most powerful telescope, such a prodigious energy barrier must surely reside at the cosmic periphery, where it acts to balance creation in rather dramatic fashion. Subsequently, it may be deduced that many currently observed quasars and star systems exist only in the form of *ghostly images* - the real sources having long since vanished in response to a fundamental law requiring the conservation of mass-energy!

THE ETERNAL UNIVERSE

Should we ask for an explanation as to why the "boundary" of the universe happens to be situated where it is, and not in some other location, it can only be concluded that volume is regulated by the quantity of spirit comprising one entire generation of "A" within the Great Pyramid of Life! In other words, whatever amount of spirit is necessary to constitute the level of Perfection, so the size of the universe must coincide with the need to express all elementary and intermediate forms in terms of a physical manifestation. *Hence, the total amount of matter in existence will be seen to be directly related to the quantity of spirit required to populate all levels of the Cosmic Pyramid!* Accordingly, with knowledge of the actual size of the universe, it will be possible to deduce the full number of "steps" of spiritual doubling or fusion which extend from the initial status of a lowly "A" to the Ultimate Goal of Perfection which we would define as God!

What are the chances of our Earth experiencing such a dramatic ending in the foreseeable future? Actually, the odds appear strongly in favor of just this happening long before life is extinguished as a consequence of solar evolution. Regardless of the size of the cosmos, it may be computed that eight times as much matter resides in the outermost half of the universe (from the point where recession is 50% that of light) as in the remaining portionall of which must undergo annihilation in one cycle of Hubble's constant. By the laws of probability, it might be argued, we are presently living on borrowed time and are long overdue!

True though this may turn out to be the immediate situation is not nearly as frightening as it might first seem. Inside the huge volume of the universe a human lifetime represents the smallest fragment of time in the overall sequence of events. Even conceding that we may now occupy a position very close to the edge, the prospects of us reaching this critical boundary are extremely slim in terms of a decade or a century. Should we substitute millions of years it would, conceivably, be entirely another matter.

Chapter 5

THE "SMALL BANG" SCENARIO

(Small Bang Vestiges in Terms of Z Redshift - The Distribution of Quasars - Quasar Luminosity by Redshift/Direction - Radiation Propagation and Cosmic Arcing - The Microwave Background.)

The value of any scientific theory lies in its ability to withstand test. Unless it is susceptible to analysis it must remain an idea rooted solely in conjecture. Most assuredly, the premise of quasars as Small Bang vestiges is a verifiable concept which invites urgent investigation.

Small Bang Vestiges in Terms of Z Redshift

With quasars defined in terms of Small Bang vestiges, it is essential to ponder this assumption in the light of observational data. What evidence is there to support the idea of a steady procession of Small Bang creations? In retrospect, it may well be suggested that, if astronomers had not been so engrossed with preconceived notions of one Big Bang, they would have been in a position to recognize certain clues. (The microwave background radiation, long considered strong evidence in support of the Big Bang concept, will shortly be seen to have an entirely different explanation.)

An initial indication was the discovery that small, loosely bound clusters of galaxies, were arranged into larger - and surprisingly uniform - swarms called superclusters. Typical separations between superclusters tend to focus upon distances of approximately half a billion or so light years. (Our own *Local Supercluster* very likely encompasses both the Virgo and Hydra-Centaurus Clouds - the two systems together having their origin in a common Small Bang creation site. Becoming highly elongated by reason of extreme rotation, the ensuing explosion must have served to eject the bulk of matter in largely opposite directions. Some 180 MLY distant, the present location of the Hydra Centaurus Cloud can be explained on the basis of a relative ejection velocity averaging only about ½% of the speed of light, with the expansion of the universe accounting for the remainder of the observed separation following a momentous explosion some 16-20 billion years ago. Almost certainly, the supergiant elliptical galaxy known as M87, in the constellation of Virgo, was once a quasar parent of our system.) This large-scale clustering and homogeneity of the universe is not at all what should be expected from a single Big Bang explosion. It is exactly what might be anticipated upon the principle of periodic Small Bang creations!

Yet another hint of a stable and eternal universe, embracing an endless procession of superdense sites, is to be found in the very existence of quasars. In fact, they are precisely what might be inferred as vestiges of Small Bang explosion sites! Not only do we have the stupendous mass/density that is so characteristic of a quasar, but the presence of a central supermassive black hole is an inevitable by-product of a Small Bang creation. (This is not to say that all cataloged quasars are genuine superdense vestiges. Inasmuch as there is somewhat of a fine dividing line between older - and less luminous - quasars and the more brilliant of the Seyfert-type galaxies, it follows that a measure of uncertainty is bound to exist. Hence, while it may be stated that every Small Bang site will indeed give rise to a quasar, exceptionally compact galaxies with very massive central black holes will also exhibit quasar-like features which could lead to cases of mistaken identity. Accordingly, there is need to establish more stringent qualifications as to quasar membership - possibly, using criteria based upon intrinsic luminosity.)

This quasar interpretation of Small Bang vestiges can be put to an interesting and revealing test. Having some knowledge of the average separations, between the centers of superclusters, it becomes possible to calculate the number of quasars compatible with such a model. Furthermore, it is feasible to compute distribution in terms of Z redshift. Uncertainties entering into the picture are posed by the necessity of having to estimate the life span of the average quasar, along with the probability that some of the less luminous quasars might really be powerful Seyfert-type galaxies seen from great distances. Possessing an exceptionally bright nucleus, with a massive black hole at its center, such a galaxy may also fluctuate in brilliance like a quasar.

Before attempting to reduce the abundance of quasars to mathematical formula, however, it is desirable to consider what effect disintegration at the edge of the universe will have upon the maximum redshift which a quasar may exhibit. For quite regardless of where a quasar or galaxy may form, within our finite expanding universe, there must be an upper limit as to how long it can continue to exist before reaching the velocity of light and suffering extinction. Subject to certain subtleties induced by proximity to the cosmic edge, this cutoff of Z redshift represents the maximum interval of time that light can remain in transit - *without either the radiation or ourselves going over the edge!*

Assuming a separation of roughly a quarter of a billion or so light years as a typical initial distance between a recent Small Bang site and the closest supercluster, it is possible to assess the implications of this figure as it applies to the total number of shells or cycles of Hubble's constant likely to constitute our physical universe. In effect, the universe may be visualized as a series of concentric shells expanding outward from a common center, with each successive shell double that of all the inner shells. In billions of light years (BLY) the radius of each successive shell, moving inward from the outer edge, is as follows: (1) 9 BLY, (2) 4.5 BLY, (3) 2.25 BLY, (4) 1.125 BLY, (5) .5625 BLY, (6) .28125 BLY. Upon this basis there will be seen to be six cycles of Hubble's constant and a minimum average separation between recent Small Bang zones and previous superdense sites (by now superclusters of galaxies) of about .28125 BLY. (See Fig. #5.)

Thus, in a period of 12 billion years, a centrally located Small Bang creation zone will have moved to a distance of about .5625 BLY and will be receding at 3.125% of the velocity of light. In two cycles of Hubble's constant it will have doubled both speed and distance, reaching a point some 1.125 BLY from the center of the universe and possessing a speed 6.25% that of light. After three cycles there will be a distance of 2.25 BLY and a velocity 12.5% that of light. With four cycles distance will be increased to 4.5 BLY and speed of recession will now be 25% that of light. Five cycles will result in a velocity of 50% and a distance of 9 BLY. Upon achieving six cycles (equivalent to $Z = 4.0$ and a transit time of 72 billion years) this same region of space will have attained the velocity of light, relative to the center of the universe, and will have moved some 18 BLY to the cosmic edge where sudden extinction awaits.

The premise of quasars being vestiges of Small Bang creation sites can, of course, be put to a rather crucial test by comparing theoretical and observational quantities - especially with regard to their relative abundance at various Z redshifts. In the last analysis, the entire problem really hinges upon an assessment of two opposing factors. For just as surely as there are factors tending to increase the likelihood of observation, so others exist which would serve to reduce the numbers of those that may be detected. Essentially, those factors contributing to increased abundance may be defined as follows:

(1) *Increase of distance.* (In effect, a twofold increase of distance is tantamount to an eightfold increase in volume of space - equivalent to an eightfold increase in numbers.)

(2) *Smaller size of Small Bang creation zone.* (In this instance, every twofold reduction in the diameter of such a zone will imply an eightfold increase in quantity.)

(3) *Longer average life span for quasars.* (Since all quasars must undergo some evolutionary change with time, it is evident that the longer they can continue to emit prodigious amounts of radiation the greater the interval of time in which they will be recognized as such.)

(4) *Increased time of light propagation.* (Due to reinstatement of the "law of addition of speeds" it now means that, in the case of extreme redshifts, we are enabled to view appreciably more than one cycle of Hubble's constant. Hence, as larger redshifts are encountered, so it is possible to observe the ghostly images of more than the actual number of existing quasars.)

In contrast to the above factors, which would facilitate detection of greater numbers of quasars, exactly the opposite effect may be assumed with a reversal of the same set of circumstances.

With Hubble's constant established at about 12 billion years in a universe with a radius of some 18 BLY, along with an inferred average separation or radius of Small Bang sites (both past and present) of the order of .28125 BLY, we are left with the task of estimating the life span of a typical quasar. Fortunately, we are not without certain clues.

As a lower limit, we must consider the fact that some quasars are known to be associated with galaxies of stars, the condensation of which would take time following an expulsion of matter from a Small Bang creation site. (At least one or two billion years would likely be the minimum required interval.) At the other extreme, it would have to be substantially less than the age of our own Milky Way and Local Supercluster, the oldest stars of which may not greatly exceed 15 billion years. Based upon the evidence at our disposal it seems logical to conclude that the average period of time, in which a quasar is clearly recognizable as such (of at least absolute magnitude -24.0), may well be of the order of about six billion years.

Utilizing this information we can now attempt to calculate the total number of quasars, visible to ourselves, in terms of specified Z redshift. A simplified formula may be expressed as follows:

$$N = \frac{VLP}{SH^2}$$

Where:

N = Total number of quasars observable up to specified Z redshift.

V = Volume of space within a radius equal to that of quasar distance in question.

S = Volume of space contained within the diameter of a typical Small Bang creation zone.

L = Life span of average quasar (in years).

H = Hubble's constant (in years).

P = Time of light propagation as a factor of Hubble's constant (in years) from quasar of specified Z redshift. (Note: "P" cannot be less than Hubble's constant.)

Upon such a theoretical basis the gradual increase in numbers of quasars at low redshifts, along with a dramatic and steady rise up to a point well below $Z = 3.0$, is exactly the combination of curve and slope required to fit observation! (See Fig. #6.) Moreover, the quantities implied at various redshifts appear to be in excellent agreement with evidence. (Predictably, the frequency of Small Bangs - within the expanse of our observable universe - is likely to be about one in every 10^5 years.)

A departure from the general slope, at higher redshifts, has long been noticed by astronomers who have chosen to interpret the entire curve in terms of subsequent condensations from a solitary Big Bang creation. Accordingly, it was assumed that the birth of quasars began slowly almost two billion years after the initial explosion - with formation proceeding at an accelerated rate until finally stabilizing some billions of years later. (The problem of explaining the equally pronounced curve below $Z = 1.0$, in which the population of quasars is seen to dwindle to zero at a distance of a little over half a billion light years, remained a rather good mystery. Why should there be none in our Local Super-cluster, while abundant only a billion or so light years away and with relatively minor difference in time of light transit?) Not only does the concept of Small Bang creation vestiges readily account for the observed curve at low redshifts, but it also affords an excellent explanation for the noted departure at high redshifts: This last curve can now receive a very different interpretation once a proper assessment has been made of the consequences of either a literal disintegration at the cosmic edge, or an equivalent effect at the boundary of our observable universe.

To understand how a sudden termination of images could produce other than an abrupt cutoff of the general slope at $Z = 4.0$, it is necessary to consider the average lifetime of a quasar as it relates to the time remaining before extinction at the edge of the observable universe intervenes. For instance, at $Z = 4.0$, where maximum redshift intercedes and imposes a theoretical cutoff, a distance of 16.62 BLY and a velocity of recession of some 92.31% that of light will be inferred. Assuming a typical quasar lifetime of about 6 billion years, it may be calculated that a distance of 4.75 BLY will be covered in this same interval of time in order to reach $Z = 4.0$. Thus it may be deduced that the aforementioned departure must begin at a distance equivalent to some 11.87 BLY (16.62 BLY - 4.75 BLY), which translates to a redshift of $Z = 1.21$. As a result, it is bound to be the very inability of the more redshifted quasars to live out their full life spans, before encountering extinction or reaching the point where speed of recession prohibits detection, which produces this departure. Essentially, those quasars with redshifts in excess of about $Z = 1.21$ will suffer a degree of extinction (or reduced detection) before they have burned long enough for their light to have contributed fully to the universal population of visible quasars. Hence, from the point where the lifetime of a quasar coincides with the transit time required to encounter extinction at the edge of the observable universe, so a reduction of numbers must ensue and become of overwhelming importance as redshifts approaching the hypothetical $Z = 4.0$ limit* are reached!

Now the very geometry of a basic Steady-state cosmology, interspersed with Small Bang creation sites, must mean that quasars (of the same age) likely possess typical separations with regard to spatial distribution. Totally against the dictates of a solitary superdense origin, if such a preferred separation factor can be substantiated it will afford even more graphic proof of an Eternal Universe.

When evaluating this inferred clustering of quasar redshifts, however, it is necessary to adopt an average separation pattern which embraces a multiple of .28125 BLY, rather than the diameter of a primordial Small Bang creation zone of the order of some .5625 BLY. The reason for this may be attributed to the manner whereby newly created "A" is introduced into the universe. Specifically, a continuous creation of "A" will facilitate a lack of synchronization with regard to the time factor in which Small Bang explosions will occur relative to each other. This *staggering of quasar births* is really tantamount to reducing redshift multiples to a figure comparable to half the distance between neighboring superclusters - representing the point at which quasars are most likely to be found relative to past superdense sites which are now mature star systems. (Were successive generations of quasars all formed at the same instant of time, with respect to both Hubble's constant and some central cosmic clock, they would in fact exhibit distance separations consistent with the .5625 BLY figure so characteristic of the diameter of Small Bang creation zones prior to their condensation.)

Unfortunately, any separation pattern will tend to be masked by a number of rather formidable factors. A variation in the sizes of Small Bang creation zones, for instance, must have a definite and obvious effect. So will a difference in the ages at which quasars are viewed. Of concern at close range, any age differential will become of major importance when more extreme distances are

---

* Redshifts, well in excess of $Z = 4.0$, are to be expected by an observer situated in close proximity to the nearby edge, due to the almost virtual entrapment of radiation at the cosmic periphery. Also, the very premise of a general bending of extragalactic light must imply enhanced transit times - beyond $Z = 4.0$ - for certain remote sources located at the other side of the universe.

involved, as it must lead to increased movement away from an initial creation site. Also compounding the problem is the deduced arcing of extragalactic radiation, along with a pronounced distortion of redshifts which is to be found in the general direction of the nearby cosmic edge. Indeed, so drastic is this last factor that the "semi-entrapment" of radiation - in the vicinity of the cosmic boundary - is capable of imparting enormous redshifts to some quasars which really emitted their light only a comparatively short distance from each other, and from where we are currently situated! In brief, any distance/velocity/redshift scale is caused to break down completely near the periphery of the universe, adding immensely to the task of evaluating quasar separations.

Nevertheless, in spite of all these obstacles, there is hope that it will eventually be possible to confirm the prediction of a common factor of separation between quasars of similar age. While a preliminary study would appear to offer encouragement, in this regard, it is imperative that a large sample be examined in depth, and in the light of what might be termed the "New Cosmology." It may well be proven that mysterious examples of quasar redshift "clumping" - previously looked upon as statistical curiosities - have a perfectly logical solution within the framework of a Steady-state/Small Bang model.

The Distribution of Quasars

Considering the fact that we see quasars as they were billions of years ago, we also see them as appearing in positions distorted by the curvature of their light as it is influenced by the expansion of the universe. By way of recapitulation, this displacement of images (or "cosmic arcing") is determined by three factors:

(1) The *time* of light transit, as implied by distance. (A longer transit time must result in increased curvature.)

(2) The *position angle* of a quasar, relative to our motion toward the edge of the universe. (The greater this angle, the greater the bending of light.)

(3) The *proximity* of an observed quasar to the outer edge, in which the curvature of radiation is seen to be enhanced with increased distance from the center of the universe.

THE ETERNAL UNIVERSE

In every instance displacement will be one *in which light is bent toward the cosmic center!* (See Fig. #5.) The inevitable question now arises, of course, as to whether observation can substantiate such a prediction.

Should we happen to be situated in a relatively central portion of the universe (with little motion toward the edge) we might expect to see no appreciable clumping of quasars, which would appear to be evenly distributed in all directions. Upon the far more logical basis of an eccentric location, and assuming the validity of our new cosmological model and revised views of light propagation, one should anticipate an unhomogeneous pattern with regard to the distribution of quasars. The standard Big Bang cosmology, on the other hand, offers two choices. With a somewhat improbable central location, a uniform distribution is again indicated. In contrast, an eccentric position would require the complete absence of all high redshift objects in one specific direction - namely, toward the nearest edge of the universe. (By the very "laws of probability," we should be situated at least 14 BLY from the cosmic center, and no further than 4 BLY from the nearby edge, since slightly more than half of all the matter in the universe is located in this latter zone.)

To date, a weakness of all quasar surveys may be ascribed to the relatively small number of QSOs catalogued, and to the somewhat less than ideal homogeneity with regard to the manner in which some quasars have been found. Nevertheless, while such unfortunate bias has yet to be negated, and is likely to persist in one form or another for years to come, it is extremely doubtful if the overall scenario will be seriously affected by current limitations. What is presently available is really tantamount to a typical sample poll, from which a great deal of useful information may be obtained concerning the structure of our dynamic universe. Indeed, rich fields of QSOs will be seen to exist in spite of preferential treatment; in fact, they were the very reason for intensive study! Likewise, regions exhibiting few quasars have been unduly avoided simply because they had already proven to be unfruitful fields.

Upon detailed analysis of a comprehensive quasar survey, published by the *European Southern Observatory,** a most in-

---

*   See *A Catalogue of Quasars and Active Nuclei (2nd Edition),* by M.-P. Veron Cetty and P. Veron, Scientific Report No. 4 - April 1985.

structive pattern is noted. Containing a total of 2,720 members (of at least absolute magnitude -23.0), it is at once evident that the vast bulk of quasars reside in two major clumpings. Not only are these two concentrations situated in exactly opposite directions of the sky, but a highly conspicuous shortage is observed at right angles to such aggregations - a distribution which is totally against the dictates of the popular Big Bang cosmology! (See Figures #7 and #8.) Moreover, when the most luminous of these quasars are considered as a group, it is revealed that an overwhelming proportion of high redshift/high luminosity QSOs are centered about the constellation of Sculptor in the Southern Hemisphere - a region which is also seen to be essentially devoid of high luminosity quasars of low redshift! In contrast, the opposite hemisphere is characterized by a mixture of high and low redshift quasars.

Although it might be thought that the center of the universe must lie in the midst of the high redshift clumping, this is most certainly not the case. Upon the basis of a Small Bang/Steady-state cosmology, and an eccentric cosmic location, the central regions of our universe should display a wide variety of redshifts. On the other hand, the nearby edge is bound to be deficient in brilliant low redshift quasars - simply because there is less room for new and highly luminous QSOs to be formed! Furthermore, a concentration of high redshift objects (toward the immediate edge) is to be expected by reason of the virtual entrapment of radiation, which allows us to view multiple generations of quasars with greatly extended light transit times. Accordingly, it will be concluded that the cosmic center is probably located near the coordinates of R.A. 13 hr and Dec. +40 degrees, near the border of the Northern Hemisphere constellations of Canes Venatici and Coma Berenices. The nearby cosmic edge is likely to reside in the general vicinity of R.A. 1 hr. and Dec. -40 degrees, very possibly within the constellation of Sculptor.

Quite inexplicable in terms of any Big Bang interpretation, the mystery of a dichotomous quasar distribution is therefore seen to have a perfectly logical solution. It is clearly much more than a coincidence that the congested central core of the universe is accompanied by a pronounced right angle shortage - a phenomenon invariably produced by the prescribed bending of extragalactic light. The prodigious edge clumping, with its preponderance of high redshift quasars, has a ready explanation upon the basis of our eccentric cosmic location and a revised concept of radiation propagation. Instead of visualizing such strongly redshifted radiation as having come from the outskirts of the universe many billions of light years away, it is really our own Milky Way which has done most of the traveling! Moving outward more than half the radius of the universe since the formation of our galactic system, we are only now encountering the light of long extinct quasars which has literally hung suspended - *almost in a state of total entrapment* - close to the cosmic edge for enormous periods of time. When we observe high redshift quasars, with light transit times of tens of billions of years, we are actually viewing very ancient images which might well be described as *celestial fossils* - the real objects having ceased to exist eons before our Earth was born! It may be presumed, in fact, that - in the direction of the nearby edge - all quasars (and most galaxies) are nothing more than ghostly apparitions of long extinct phenomena!

Quasar Luminosity by Redshift/Direction

With quasar luminosity acknowledged to be a function of age, it is expedient to assess the distribution of quasar luminosity versus redshift over the expanse of the entire sky. In searching out high liminosity QSOs of all visual magnitudes, and adopting a lower limit of absolute magnitude -29.0 and a redshift minimum of $Z = 2.5$, we find a total of 65 qualifying quasars in the aforementioned European Southern Observatory catalogue. Upon plotting these objects on the two hemisphere charts (Fig. #7 and Fig. #8), it is at once evident that a preponderance (41 to 24) is centered upon the coordinates of the inferred nearby cosmic edge. In point of fact, almost 2/3rds of these exceptional QSOs are situated in an area comprising only 1/3rd of the heavens! This translates to a ratio of more than 5 to 1 in favor of an unhomogeneous distribution. (When redshifts of at least -30.0 are substituted, the ratio is increased to 6.5 to 1.)

Of equal significance is a pronounced shortage of low redshift quasars of high luminosity residing in the vicinity of this same nearby cosmic edge, *where they are quite conspicuous by their absence!* Most abundant elsewhere, they are almost totally absent in this one particular direction. (See Fig. #7 and Fig. #8.)

THE ETERNAL UNIVERSE

Needless to say, an explanation is demanded for yet another strange anomaly. Impossible to answer in terms of any Big Bang cosmology, this peculiar shortage will now be conceded to arise by reason of our highly eccentric cosmic location, as reduced volume of space acts to impose a rather drastic restriction as to where (and in what direction) luminous quasars of recent vintage may be formed. In this one preferred direction of the sky, it must surely follow that the last light of many neighboring quasars has already passed us enroute to more central regions of our universe!

Valuable insight into this most biased distribution may be obtained through analysis of the quasar sample following its division into a succession of redshift bins. Expressed in multiples of Z = .200, and considering an edge group member to be one residing in this same 1/3rd portion of the total sky, we are enabled to construct the data conveyed in Figure #9. A truly amazing picture emerges. With virtually zero difference at Z = .200, substantial excess luminosity (away from the edge) is quickly encountered and observed to peak in the vicinity of Z = .400 - *from whence the luminosity differential is seen to proceed in the opposite direction!* Effecting a complete reversal between Z = 1.80 and Z = 2.00, a progressive surplus of intrinsic luminosity (in the direction of the edge) will be noted to characterize the remainder of the higher redshift bins. Nor is this variation of minor consequence. From Z = .400 to the limit of detection, the combined bin differential average translates to a brightness factor of some 360% - a factor which is direction oriented! Even when modified appreciably, by considering only the total average luminosity of all quasars within this same spread of redshifts, we are left with an overall luminosity surplus that is 174% higher in the direction of the nearby edge. Most assuredly, this striking pattern is not at all compatible with an explosive Big Bang origin!

In the process of explaining this remarkable observation it will be seen that we are now in a position to verify a proffered solution for a major weakness inherent in previous versions of Steady-state cosmology - namely, the lack of conservation of mass-energy. Indeed, very graphic confirmation of this momentous prediction (involving annihilation at the cosmic periphery) is already at hand in the evidence afforded by Figure #9, in which there is clearly a marked tendency of intrinsic luminosities and extreme redshifts to be noticeably higher in the direction of the nearby edge. Inasmuch as the energy output of a quasar is bound to diminish with age (typically, a hundredfold reduction may be inferred in the span of about 10 billion years), as it slowly evolves into a giant galaxy with a supermassive black hole core, it follows that *higher luminosity is also a definite indication of youth!* But why should they be younger? This is surely the question which begs an answer. The obvious conclusion, of course, is that something must be preventing normal aging of quasars in this one region of the sky! Invariably,*it is a selective effect imposed by premature disintegration at the boundary of our physical universe* - from whence an equivalence of mass-energy is subsequently reincarnated as infinitesimal quanta in the great voids of outer space!

Radiation Propagation and Cosmic Arcing

In order to acquire deeper insight into the magnitude of our eccentric cosmic location, it is desirable to contemplate how propagation of radiation is restricted to a theoretical maximum of $Z = 4.00$. With the constant outward pressure of cosmic expansion tending to become ever more efficient at inducing radiation to undergo "arcing," as the boundary of the universe is approached, it is really a matter of asking at what distance from the edge will radiation succumb to total arcing. If there is in truth a basic $Z = 4.00$ limit, a comparatively narrow "shell" or "inclusion zone" must exist at the cosmic periphery - *from which point it is very difficult for radiation to escape and reach the more central regions of our universe!*

Assessment of this "inclusion zone" is best grasped by visualizing the path of radiation as it streaks toward us from the opposite side of the universe. Fighting against a strong outward flowing stream of quanta during initial stages of its journey, it will spend tens of billions of years merely to reach the cosmic center. Thereafter, it will experience a "tailwind" and is enabled to cover the remaining 18 BLY in a period of barely more than 12 billion years! (See Fig. #5.) The total distance covered in an interval of 72 billion years (equivalent to a redshift of $Z = 4.00$) is some 35.4375 BLY. Thus it may be deduced that the depth of this "inclusion zone" is of the order of .5625 BLY - a figure which turns out to be the same as the distance across a typical Small Bang creation zone!

At this point it might appear as though we are faced with somewhat of a paradox. In terms of velocity of recession the inferred "inclusion zone" cutoff is indicative of a recession speed some 96.875% that of light, implying that any radiation reaching us from the opposite side of the universe (at a distance of 35.4375 BLY) must have started out with an effective approach velocity of about 3.125% light speed. On the other hand, normal translation of $Z = 4.00$ gives a recession velocity of 92.31% and a distance of 16.62 BLY, seemingly posing an outright contradiction. However, what must be realized is that even the revised Redshift/Time/Velocity/Distance scale must break down to an observer residing in the vicinity of the cosmic edge! (It will be noted that the time aspect remains valid; it is only distance and velocity which are negated due to widely varying circumstances under which radiation encounters outward flowing quanta.)

It will therefore be acknowledged that the redshift/distance curve of Figure #4 really depicts the scenario to be expected from a location at the center of the universe. A more realistic view, conceding our highly eccentric cosmic position, may be found in Figure #10. The aforementioned luminosity reversal, between $Z = 1.80$ and $Z = 2.00$, will now be seen to represent the point where time of propagation overtakes distance - beyond which a rapid increase in transit time is effected with only a nominal increase of distance! In turn, this permits detection of multiple cycles of cosmic renewal and enhancement of the number of premature quasar extinctions observed in the direction of the immediate edge - a degree of bias precluded elsewhere due to arcing away of a higher percentage of light from remote sources at the other side of the universe. (While the absolute magnitudes of high redshift quasars may thus warrant an upward assessment - due to increased distance - it will not detract from the picture of a direction oriented luminosity bias.)

Although certainly a factor to be considered, any time delay that is experienced by radiation - as it interacts with the infinitesimal quanta of space - will likely be of relatively minor importance. Nevertheless, it must serve to augment many redshifts (from remote sources situated at the far side of the universe) beyond any theoretical $Z = 4.00$ limit. With regard to detection of extreme redshifts, in the direction of the nearby boundary, it may be postulated that an observer located inside the immediate "exclusion zone" could expect to find redshifts considerably in excess of $Z = 4.00$ - but only at the expense of our residing near the very edge of the universe itself! (This prediction follows from the premise that the degree of arcing hinges quite strongly upon the *distance traveled* - in the sense that a very short transit will permit little arcing. Accordingly, this must imply that extreme redshifts - from radiation virtually trapped at the edge - may be observed by those who are actually poised at the brink of extinction!)

Were one to proceed upon the rash assumption that we are presently situated some billions of light years from the periphery of the universe, it may be reasoned that the nearby edge should be deficient of high redshift images - simply because the vast majority of such radiation would be induced to arc away before it could reach us. (By analogy, this arcing might be likened unto a lone paddler sitting at the stern of a long canoe and attempting to make headway into the face of a very strong wind. Without any ballast in the bow it requires only a slight deviation in order for the wind to catch the canoe and force it to arc away from its original course. Moreover, the greater this angle becomes the more susceptible it must be to further arcing.) In this instance about the only light that we might expect to encounter would be modest redshifts from objects located toward the innermost limits of the nearby "inclusion zone." Sources capable of producing extreme redshifts would have to reside very close to the cosmic boundary, where arcing must intercede to prevent the escape of radiation. Subsequently, a study of redshifts, in the general direction of the edge, should prove most informative.

The picture to emerge is somewhat less than reassuring. The entire region of the edge is seen to be heavily populated by high redshift quasars; in fact, it contains a large concentration of the most extreme redshifts discovered to date! In order for us to detect these redshifts, which are indicative of light transit times involving tens of billions of years, *we must currently be situated well inside the confines of an "inclusion zone"* - a distance inferred to be some .5625 BLY in depth! It is our very proximity to the edge which allows us to intercept such radiation before it has been subjected to appreciable arcing. Indeed, since arcing is essentially a product of distance traveled, rather than of transit time, it follows that failure to find a region of the immediate edge free of extreme redshifts means that we have reached *this same point in space* where images of long extinct quasars have been largely unaffected by arcing! Invariably, we must now occupy a position perhaps no further than millions of light years from the edge!

THE ETERNAL UNIVERSE

The Microwave Background

In the opinion of most scientists the microwave background radiation originated, some billions of years ago, in the intense heat and density of a Big Bang explosion. It is further believed that expansion of the universe has served to reduce highly energetic radiation to an observed wavelength peak of about 1 mm which, in turn, has been translated to a temperature of close to 3 degrees K. There is every reason to suspect that this concept is both illogical and erroneous; in fact, it bespeaks an uncritical assessment of current nebulous views of radiation.

The very idea of stretching wavelengths - from the realm of high energy gamma rays into the region of enormously weaker microwaves - poses a rather vexing contradiction with a basic tenet of physics which demands conservation of mass-energy. Totally ignoring the issue of particle mass, it fails to explain how such entities as electron/positron combinations (gamma rays) can incur a drastic reduction of mass simply because the universe is expanding! (Upon the basis of the "New Cosmology" every component of creation is seen to possess mass, or ability to commune gravitationally - a property which may be negated, as in the case of the elusive neutrino and radiation in general, solely because of extreme relative motion at the speed of light, since this is the velocity by which gravitation is propagated.) Consequently, it is inconceivable that cosmic expansion can have any direct effect upon the actual mass-energy congealed into corpuscles of radiation. All that it can do is to impose a reduction of flux and of frequency (wave crests per unit time) by reason of Doppler shift. *However produced, the microwave background radiation cannot undergo any substantial change from time of formation to detection!*

Even conceeding that some microwave radiation (as such) may escape from Small Bang creation sites, the low energy level and remarkably isotropic nature of this phenomenon is suggestive of an entirely different origin as a primary source. What is surely indicated is an homogeneous production mechanism, more characteristic of the *absolute zero* of outer space, than of the incredibly high temperature of a primordial fireball! The most probable scenario to emerge involves elementary matter forms strewn throughout the expanse of space, where the chief source of energy which may be encountered is the larger "repulsive" quanta responsible for the expansion of the universe. The problem becomes one of explaining how exceedingly minute gravitational quanta are absorbed and, subsequently, emitted as more massive microwave radiation. In essence, *the microwave background reflects the average temperature of matter in the cold isolation of extragalactic space!*

While a great deal remains to be explored in depth, it is logical to infer that (in the immediate vicinity of relatively massive material particles) quanta of a certain size range and flux will infrequently exist in mutual association long enough to enter into a degree of fusion. When the inevitable expulsion occurs, it could well be in the form of discrete corpuscles with masses characteristic of the microwave region of the spectrum. (It is to be expected that expulsion of absorbed quanta, in the almost absolute zero of space, will not be so abrupt as would be the case at higher temperature.) Although only a small fraction of ingested quanta is likely to congeal into such radiation, what is produced will be propagated back and forth among components of the interstellar medium. Thus a universal sea of microwave radiation (centered about a wavelength of close to 1 mm) may be presumed to arise through creation in the halos of isolated material particles, rather than originating in a superdense explosion!

Since passage through a uniform field of microwave radiation is bound to exhibit a Doppler shift, extensive measurements have been made in order to determine the direction of our motion through space. It is reported that the temperature of the microwave background is slightly higher in the direction of the constellation of Leo; while it is less by an identical amount in exactly the opposite direction of the sky, in the constellation of Aquarius. This has been interpreted to mean that the Milky Way, along with other members of our Local Group, shares a common motion (about 520 km/s) toward Leo. On the surface, this revelation would seem to conflict with impressive evidence that our entire region of space is currently moving (at some 99.985% light speed, as we shall soon see) toward the nearest cosmic edge, which is believed to lie in the direction of Sculptor. What may be wondered is why observation appears to indicate movement in almost exactly the *opposite* direction!

To resolve this paradox it is essential to contemplate certain aspects of cosmic expansion in the light of the "New

THE ETERNAL UNIVERSE

Cosmology." Inasmuch as absorption and emission of quanta cannot occur in zero time, it is most logical to infer that a massive galaxy will resist acceleration more than individual material particles. Indeed, in order to impart motion to vast star systems, it is necessary for the impetus of "repulsive" quanta to be transferred from atom to atom - a somewhat less than instantaneous process as galaxy components are held together by gravitational attraction. It follows, subsequently, that this time lag will enable outward bound radiation to have a slight advantage over similar corpuscles attempting to propagate toward us from the direction of the nearby edge. In effect, any lag in our Milky Way's outward acceleration is tantamount to reducing the Doppler shift of incoming quanta (from the vicinity of the cosmic center) - thereby explaining why the microwave background radiation is observed to be a trifle warmer toward the center of the universe.

The small discrepancy between microwave observations and quasar distribution, as a means of determining our orientation with respect to the cosmic center and nearby edge, would appear to have a ready answer. It may well be ascribed to residual orbital momentum stemming from the Small Bang which gave us birth! It would, in fact, be rather surprising if no vestige at all remained of the strong initial rotary motion of matter - now comprising our Local Supercluster - following its origin as expelled hydrogen (and helium) atoms from the region of a rapidly swirling supermassive black hole creation site. In all probability, it is prudent to look upon this apparent drift (toward Leo) as a very minor *secondary* motion, with expansion of the universe still responsible for a much faster large-scale exodus of our general region of space toward a point which is presumed to lie within the constellation of Sculptor.

Established precepts are often difficult to refute. The instinctive reluctance of man to admit acceptance of falsehood all too frequently precludes unbiased analysis of alternate views. In negating this last remnant of support for a superdense cosmology, it is clear that evidence against the Big Bang model is now so overwhelming that a parallel exists with the state of affairs which prevailed during the pioneering days of Copernicus, Kepler and Galileo. It is to be hoped that science will soon recognize the futility of attempting to preserve an outworn concept and begin to explore new horizons. The rewards will surely exceed all expectation.

Chapter 6

OUR PROXIMITY TO THE COSMIC EDGE

(D/R Arcing and Superluminal Expansion - Luminous Bridges and Cosmic Arcing - "Quantization" of Redshifts - Redshifts as Distance Indicators - Discordant Redshifts and the Cosmic Edge - Other Examples of Discordant Redshifts - Summary.)

As a consequence of postulating an annihilation factor, sufficient to offset new creation, we are confronted with a prediction that is positively mind-boggling. Although the odds of our striking such a fateful cosmic barrier - during the brief span of a human lifetime - appear to be overwhelmingly prohibitive, it is clearly a premise which demands urgent investigation. Never, in all history, have astronomers been handed a more pressing challenge than to determine our present location with respect to the nearby edge of the universe.

In a classic instance of serendipity, there is reason to suspect that this issue may receive a measure of clarification through a study of certain celestial anomalies which have recently surfaced, and which would appear to cast doubt as to the credibility of a fundamental scientific precept. Specifically, the question of redshifts now looms as a highly controversial topic, with serious anomalies threatening to undermine their usage as extragalactic distance indicators.* There are grounds for believing that much of this confusion arises from an erroneous concept of radiation propagation, and through failure to recognize a distance/repulsion (D/R) factor inherent in the phenomenon of gravitation.

Discussion of these highly relevant anomalies, in the light of the "New Cosmology," follows.

---

* An informative treatise of anomalous redshifts is to be found in a book by the eminent astronomer, Halton C. Arp. Published in 1987 by Interstellar Media, this valuable work is entitled *Quasars, Redshifts and Controversies.*

THE ETERNAL UNIVERSE

D/R Arcing and Superluminal Expansion

Impressive statistics have been advanced which clearly indicate that a disproportionately large number of quasars are to be found in close angular proximity to relatively nearby massive galaxies. Inexplicable upon the basis of traditional views, such an association suggests a physical connection which would be incompatible with the principle of redshifts serving as reliable distance indicators. It therefore remains to be explained how this anomaly can be resolved in the face of strong conflicting evidence that at least some quasars are at distances which are essentially commensurate with their redshifts.

Notwithstanding that the cosmic aberration factor (as outlined in the "New Cosmology") predicts a dichotomous clumping of quasar images, it is evident that this convergence of QSOs into two major concentrations will be insufficient to account for observation. Yet another factor must somehow be involved - *one which would permit intervening galaxies to focus incoming quasar radiation toward such centers of mass!* In all probability, it is the proposed D/R factor which is responsible for creating a scenario of high redshift quasars seemingly associated with low redshift galaxies.

Just as a general outward flowing of the universe may cause a large-scale displacement of images toward the cosmic center, so a massive intervening galaxy is able to induce small-scale curvature in the path of radiation approaching from a more remote source - in this instance, curvature *away* from the less distant concentration of mass! However, the very action of "repulsive" quanta pushing against such approaching radiation must ensure that whatever does reach us will do so from a somewhat different angle - namely, *from a direction considerably closer to the intervening galaxy!* (See Figure #11.) Subsequently, the apparent overabundance of quasars - in angular proximity to major galaxies - is really an illusion produced by D/R arcing, and this hitherto unrecognized aspect of gravitation is thus seen responsible for still another example of celestial deception.

This very principle of "galactic arcing" of images is likely at the roots of the mystery of superluminal expansion, which has resisted a satisfactory explanation in spite of several elaborate attempts. Such a problem first surfaced when outbursts of radio emissions were studied over a time interval of some years. To the consternation of observers, many sources seemed to have ejection velocities well beyond the speed of light! (By way of example, one outburst in the quasar 3C273 was revealed to exhibit an apparent expansion velocity almost ten times that of light itself!) We may now venture a solution based upon this same ability of the D/R factor to so bend incoming radiation as to make ejected radio lobes appear *closer* to their point of origin! With the passage of time (and increased separation) it must follow that the strength of the D/R factor - in terms of ability to induce arcing - will quickly get out of synchronization with the angle of separation needed to reflect an accurate picture of recession. (According to prescribed theory, a fourfold increase of distance will result in a twofold increase of repulsion: whereas gravitational attraction is characterized by a fourfold reduction of force with a twofold increase of distance.) Inasmuch as the flux of repulsive quanta is also a function of mass or strength of gravitational attraction, *it will be seen that as a radio lobe moves away from its source a point must be reached where the D/R factor will be less effective in inducing arcing!* With time, reduced arcing must cause such lobes to appear further apart (and closer to their true angular positions) than what might be accounted for by genuine velocity of expansion - an effect which is magnified greatly by extreme line of sight distance.

Luminous Bridges and Cosmic Arcing

Among the many astronomical anomalies which have been uncovered are instances where luminous bridges appear to physically connect two objects of widely differing redshift, thereby negating the worth of extragalactic redshifts in formulating any distance/velocity scale. There is now every reason to believe that a solution to such enigmas may be found in the concept of *cosmic arcing,* as imposed by the D/R factor responsible for our expanding universe.

Perhaps the most notable example of a luminous bridge involves a galaxy known as NGC 4319 (Z = 1,700 km/s) and the quasar Markarian 205 (Z = 21,000 km/s). Located at the coordinates of R.A. 12 hr 21', and +75 deg. 45' Dec., the quasar is situated almost due south of the galaxy. Close examination of this pair reveals a narrow but quite distinct connecting bridge. At first glance, this would appear to afford irrefutable proof of physical proximity, being located at the edge of the halo of gas and stars surrounding the galaxy's nucleus.

It is highly probable that this illuminated bridge is a product of cosmic arcing. In the course of having its radiation arced toward the center of the universe, the distant quasar's light will be seen to have passed behind the nucleus before emerging in the vicinity of the galactic halo. During this grazing passage any intervening matter will be light-enhanced, in the form of a narrow illuminated beam or path, by the relatively intense radiation of the quasar. It may well be much more than a coincidence that this bridge points precisely toward the cosmic center!

Incidently, this general deflection of images - toward the center of the universe - may explain a curious distribution of quasars about the galaxy M82. (The coordinates of this system are R.A. 9 hr 51', Dec. +69 deg. 55'.) No less than four QSOs appear to lie in a somewhat narrow cone stretching to the southeast of the galaxy - a direction which just happens to coincide exactly with a line extending toward the cosmic center, at R.A. 13 hr and +40 deg. Dec.! It is difficult to refute the inference that, in such an instance, we are looking at an example of cosmic arcing reinforced by a more localized galactic focusing of images.

"Quantization" of Redshifts

Adding to the confusion of astronomers is data which would seem to establish a rather peculiar pattern in galaxy redshifts. To the dismay and astonishment of many scientists, it has been disclosed that the redshifts of galaxy cluster members tend to congregate about certain discrete values - implying that an unknown subtlety is involved in the creation of such redshifts.* Understandably, this revelation has served to add impetus to the controversy regarding the credibility of redshifts as distance indicators.

Although much remains to be studied in depth, it is conceivable that the inferred D/R factor is capable of shedding a degree of light upon this issue. Not only does the repulsive aspect

---

* See *Quantized Galaxy Redshifts*, by W. G. Tifft and W. J. Cocke, Sky & Telescope January, 1987.

of gravitation produce an expanding universe, by pushing galaxy clusters apart, but in the process of interacting with radiation it must also imprint a *time delay* fully commensurate with this intervention. In effect, when radiation approaches our Milky Way system it encounters a specific strength - related to the mass of our Galaxy - of "repulsive" quanta, which acts to *increase the time of transit.* (The greater the mass of a receiving galaxy the greater must be this retardation factor that is imposed upon incoming radiation, as absorption and emission of quanta cannot occur in zero time.) Thus it will be seen that our own Milky Way is responsible for literally imprinting a *specific* degree of time retardation (or redshift) upon all extragalactic radiation.

This interpretation can be put to an interesting test. Upon the basis of theory, radiation received from low mass galaxies should be somewhat more redshifted than from equidistant high mass systems - simply because the strength of "repulsive" quanta emitted from the more massive galaxies will be greater. In turn, this stronger flow will tend to facilitate the propagation of outward bound radiation in the face of an opposing flow streaming from our own system. Analysis of the redshifts of nearby galaxy clusters affords excellent confirmation of this prediction. In the M31 (Local Group) and M81 cluster, both of which have been subjected to close scrutiny, all 21 major companions (of relatively low mass) have been found to possess higher redshifts than their more dominant cluster constituents! The chance of this being an accidental occurrence is so incredibly slim that it must lend strong support to the principle of a D/R factor.

There is reason to suspect that a noted "quantization" of redshifts among members of such galaxy clusters as Abell 262 and the Coma cluster, for example, is similarly rooted in effects of gravitational repulsion. To the puzzlement of observers, it has been discovered that different types of galaxies (lying at roughly the same distance) display noticeably different redshifts. Those of high luminosity and concentrated mass tend to possess lower redshifts than their less brilliant and less massive neighbors! It may now be suggested that this peculiarity affords further confirmation of the D/R factor at work. In essence, the overall flux of "repulsive" quanta (flowing from galaxies) will impart very distinctive patterns with regard to time of light propagation - hence, to redshift. (The magnitude of this effect would imply that redshifts beyond $Z = 4.00$ may not be as uncommon as might otherwise be thought, since a lengthy transit of radiation is bound to involve numerous encounters with discrete concentrations of "repulsive" quanta - leading to an appreciable increase in time of propagation.)

Yet another cause of seemingly "quantized" redshifts may be related to geometrical effects inherent in the "New Cosmology." By reason of this hitherto unforeseen repulsive factor many galaxies will be induced to exhibit hollow globular structuring within the confines of an overall supercluster, as the D/R factor acts to push such members to separations consistent with age and mass. Viewed from afar, a "bubble-like" sphere may be expected to present three distinct instances of redshift clumping. In addition to those foreground systems attempting to approach us due to gravitational repulsion, so an opposing background swarm will be receding (at higher speed) from the opposite side of such an expanding "bubble" configuration. Another above average concentration will take the form of a dichotomous right angle distribution that is intermediate in distance between these two extremes. Accordingly, a majority of galaxies will appear to portray characteristics of a "quantized" nature, as the factor of gravitational repulsion is permitted rather graphic expression over distances measured in tens of millions of light years.

Redshifts as Distance Indicators

To assess the worth of extragalactic redshifts as distance indicators, it is helpful to review certain fundamentals implicit in the revised concept of light propagation. First and foremost, a redshift is a true measure of the *time* that has elapsed between emission and eventual detection - quite regardless of direction and any conceivable form of intervention experienced by radiation enroute. In order to convert time into distance it is essential that the factor of cosmic expansion be taken into consideration, as radiation is caused to propagate at the velocity of light *relative to the moving field in which it is embedded!* With direction and eccentricity of our cosmic location so regulating the approach of radiation, we are led to contemplate such issues as luminosity and angular displacement in terms of redshift.

The luminosity of an object is a measure of the number of photons received in unit time. Assuming no intervention, the traditional inverse-square law will apply to the actual distance between source and observer's "location" at the time of light emission. In this instance "location" is defined as that region of space which, in compliance with the dictates of cosmic expansion, would intercept such radiation in the interval of time reflected by redshift - regardless of whether this region of space is occupied by receiver's world at the moment of emission! Restated slightly, with "location" situated in the direction of the cosmic center, distance will depict the time required for expansion to move it to the position of a source residing toward the edge. With regard to a source located at the other side of the universe, distance will express the propagation of radiation through changing flows of quanta. (After passing through the cosmic center a "headwind" will be replaced by a "tailwind.")

The angular displacement of an object is analogous to luminosity, also being commensurate with the inverse-square law applied over the distance between source and receiver's "location" - within an expanding universe - at time of light emission. Accordingly, angular size will not change with an observer's proximity to the cosmic edge, and will always exhibit the same relationship to distance as luminosity.

Extragalactic redshifts, however, while affording an accurate view of elapsed time, are seen to be highly susceptible to misinterpretation when an attempt is made to convert measurements to velocity of recession and distance - leading to numerous instances of confusion and outright contradiction with regard to a variety of celestial associations.

Discordant Redshifts and the Cosmic Edge

This very tendency to produce anomalous redshifts offers a much needed opportunity to more accurately deduce our present position with respect to the nearby edge of the universe. If one is able to estimate the true line of sight separation of two gravitationally interacting systems, in the direction of the cosmic edge, it should be possible to calculate their distance as a function of light transit time from their respective redshifts. In effect, a relatively small linear separation - in close proximity to the edge - is capable of displaying a highly discordant redshift. It therefore becomes prudent to examine as many of these interacting systems as possible, in expectation that a truly plausible and consistent agreement as to distance will be forthcoming.

One especially promising candidate association is that of NGC 7603, a large Seyfert galaxy with a smaller companion system evidently attached by a curving filament of luminous stars and gas. The redshift of the larger galaxy is indicative of a traditional recession velocity of some 8,700 km/s; while that of the smaller galaxy is 17,000 km/s. If we tentatively place the Milky Way at a current distance of 3 MLY from the cosmic edge, the effective approach speed of incoming radiation (from the direction of the edge) is likely of the order of 1.667×10^{-4} that of light. With radiation transit times of 522 MY and 1.02 BY, respectively, one may calculate that NGC 7603 had to be 2.914 MLY from the edge at the time its light began the journey to Earth. For the more distant companion galaxy a figure of 2.835 MLY may be computed, which gives a separation of about 79,000 LY between the two systems. (It will be noted that a relatively modest change in our own position must be greatly magnified when translated into separation of two such interacting systems - thus imposing a strict limitation upon any permissible estimate of our proximity to the cosmic edge!)

Another rather promising association consists of an open spiral galaxy known as AM 2006-295 (redshift 7,230 km/s) and its elongated companion (redshift 29,580 km/s), which appears to lie midway between (and behind) the nucleus and an arm of the larger spiral system. Again assuming our Milky Way to be situated some 3 MLY from the cosmic edge, we may calculate the distances of these galaxies upon the basis of light transit times of 483 MY and 1.82 BY, respectively. The figures which may be derived are 2.921 MLY from the edge for AM 2006-295, and 2.712 MLY for the companion galaxy. Hence, a separation of 209,000 LY will be inferred to exist between the two systems - a distance which (ignoring redshift) appears to be in reasonable agreement in all other respects with optical observation. (Indeed, without such an explanation the angular displacement of the higher redshift member must imply a size which - in terms of the traditional velocity/distance scale - would make it unrealistically large!)

Upon the basis of a 3 MLY figure as our present distance from the cosmic edge, statistics concerning a number of other probable interacting systems (lying in the vicinity of the edge) are as follows:

THE ETERNAL UNIVERSE

Where:
  R = Implied redshift.
  T = Time of light propagation to Milky Way.
  D = Distance from cosmic edge at time of light emission.

NGC 1232

Main Galaxy:
(R = 1,776 km/s; T = 107 MY: D = 2.982 MLY)
Companion System:
(R = 6,552 km/s; T = 393 MY; D = 2.935 MLY)

Inferred line of sight separation of galaxy pair is 47,000 LY. (Traditional redshift separation is 287 MLY.)

Incidently, a logical explanation is forthcoming for a second apparent companion to NGC 1232. Displaying a redshift of some 28,000 km/s, this compact object would seem to shine through the disk of the nearby galaxy, which should serve to redden it considerably. To the surprise of many astronomers, it is observed to be quite blue in color! There is now every reason to suspect that it is indeed a distant background system which, due to pressure of encounters with vast swarms of extragalactic "repulsive" quanta, has had its light bent in such a manner as to project an image in front of the lower redshift galaxy's spiral arm. Most assuredly, this proffered explanation is able to resolve a mystery which must otherwise stand in flat contradiction to established precepts.

AM 0328-222

Main Galaxy:
(R = 1,800 km/s; T = 108 MY; D = 2.982 MLY)
Companion System:
(R = 19,700 km/s; T = 1.182 BY; D = 2.809 MLY)

Inferred line of sight separation of galaxy pair is 173,000 LY. (Traditional redshift separation is 1.07 BLY.)

AM 059-4024

THE ETERNAL UNIVERSE

Main Galaxy:
(R = 6,730 km/s; T = 404 MY; D = 2.933 MLY)
Companion System:
(R = 16,400 km/s; T = 984 MY; D = 2.840 MLY)

Inferred line of sight separation of galaxy pair is 93,000 LY.
(Traditional redshift separation is 582 MLY.)

AM 2054-221

Main Galaxy:
(R = 10,400 km/s; T = 624 MY; D = 2.898 MLY)
Companion System:
(R = 46,860 km/s; T = 2.81 BY; D = 2.566 MLY)

Inferred line of sight separation of galaxy pair is 332,000 LY.
(Traditional redshift separation is 2.19 BLY.)

In actuality, the aforementioned figures must receive adjustment due to the influence of discrete D/R sources, which will serve to enhance all redshifts. For instance, the "repulsive" quanta that is constantly being emitted from our own Milky Way must impose a specific measure of retardation upon incoming radiation, increasing redshifts and changing statistics to a certain degree. Similarly, in the case of dominant galaxies with minor companions, the D/R factor will favor an increase in redshift of the less massive companion - leading to an overestimation of any deduced separation. (While necessitating some modification of figures, this is likely to be of relatively minor consideration when compared to the overall outward flowing of the universe, and we are thus enabled to infer a reasonably accurate picture as to the eccentricity of our cosmic location.)

Although a figure of 3 MLY may not be an unreasonable estimate of our present distance from the cosmic edge, it is desirable to contemplate other possibilities. (See Appendix #3.) A distance greater than 5 MLY would seem to imply separations that are excessive for some systems; while a figure of less than 1 MLY could raise a problem with at least one of the examples. In particular, it would take a very recent chance encounter among components of AM 2006-295 to explain a separation lower than 69,600

THE ETERNAL UNIVERSE

LY, without producing more obvious signs of gravitational disturbance. On the other hand, a separation of some 139,200 LY would likely be acceptable for this pair of galaxies - thereby permitting our Milky Way to be situated at least as close to the edge as 2 MLY. It is to be expected that additional investigation of such systems will reduce any existing uncertainty.

On the whole, it may be deduced that available evidence points to our now occupying a position rather close to the edge of the universe - very possibly, no further than some 1 to 5 million light years from the fate which surely awaits us at the cosmic periphery! (Upon making a tentative allowance for "quantized" galactic effects, the weight of such statistics would seem to favor an estimate much closer to the lower figure.)

In view of the widespread "compression of images," in the direction of the cosmic edge, it may well be asked why there are not more reported instances of discordant redshifts among cluster members. Quite simply, the answer would seem to be that such instances *do* exist; but they are generally unnoticed because many redshift differences are actually so great that they appear to require membership in other galaxy clusters! It is only when close angular proximity is noted that the issue of anomalous redshifts is raised. (Also a contributing factor is the reluctance of many astronomers to seek evidence which would challenge the credibility of accepted views involving the redshift/distance scale!)

Other Examples of Discordant Redshifts

Although a high preponderence of discordant redshifts are to be found in the direction of the nearby edge, there are a number of anomalies - toward the cosmic center - which invite discussion. Perhaps the most impressive example discovered to date is that of the remarkable chain of galaxies known as VV 172 (R.A. 11 hr 29', Dec. +71 deg. 6'). While four members possess redshifts ranging from 15,673 to 16,252 km/s, the fifth system exhibits a rather discordant 37,062 km/s. Since visual observation would lead one to assume that they are all members of the same cluster, an explanation is clearly desired.

Upon the basis of a revised concept of light propagation, it follows that radiation - from the direction of the cosmic center - is capable of imparting a somewhat distorted view of distance as a function of redshift. For instance, due to expansion of the universe, it will be seen that radiation is able to propagate outward (from the center) to a distance of 18 BLY in a period of only 12 BY; while at more extreme redshifts the opposite is true, in the sense that far more time than distance must be involved as such radiation must struggle against outward pressure merely to reach the center. Thus it is possible for some systems to display a modified reverse "compression effect" - whereby they are actually further away than what would otherwise be indicated by their redshifts. In turn, this extended distance must facilitate instances of cosmic arcing, causing images to be displaced in both angular and line of sight configuration.

In the case of VV 172 we are probably dealing with only a modest linear adjustment, but an appreciable amount of angular displacement toward the center of the universe. It is quite conceivable that the discordant member of this system has had its light bent in such a way as to cause it to appear as a fifth component in this unusual string of galaxies. In fact, it is to be expected that the phenomenon of a D/R force must produce many seemingly bizarre associations, including the much publicized Seyfert's Sextet and Stephan's Quintet - configurations defying a traditional interpretation, but which have a logical answer in terms of the "New Cosmology." (Seyfert's Sextet, in which one galaxy member is revealed to possess a redshift almost 16,000 km/s higher than the others, may simply be viewed as a classic example of cosmic arcing so displacing an image as to create a spurious interloper.)

Stephan's Quintet, however, poses an intriguing example of anomalous redshifts. Located at somewhat less than a right angle from the cosmic edge (R.A. 22 hr 34', Dec. +34 deg. 0'), this group should really be looked upon as edge inhabitants which have been subjected to considerable arcing. Three of the systems possess redshifts of 6,700 km/s. A fourth has been measured at 5,700 km/s; while the remaining galaxy exhibits a redshift of only 800 km/s - seemingly in complete disagreement with the others and contrary to all signs of gravitational interaction. Also adding to the overall scenario is the presence (some 20' of arc away) of a large neighboring spiral galaxy known as NGC 7331, with a redshift similar to that of the low redshift member of the quintet. In turn, this major system would seem to have three small companions of redshifts

6,300, 6,400 and 6,900 km/s. When it is further considered that there exists a diffuse bridge of radio-emitting material between NGC 7331 and Stephan's Quintet, the entire picture begins to resemble a celestial zoo.

If our Milky Way is indeed at a current distance of roughly 3 MLY from the cosmic edge, it is instructive to contemplate the following statistics for this peculiar configuration:

Stephan's Quintet:

NGC 7320	(R = 800 km/s;	T = 48 MY;	D = 2.992 MLY)
NGC 7318B	(R = 5,700 km/s;	T = 342 MY;	D = 2.943 MLY)
NGC 7318A	(R = 6,700 km/s;	T = 402 MY;	D = 2.933 MLY)
NGC 7317	(R = 6,700 km/s;	T = 402 MY;	D = 2.933 MLY)
NGC 7319	(R = 6,700 km/s;	T = 402 MY;	D = 2.933 MLY)

Inferred line of sight separation between:

NGC 7320 and NGC 7318B is 49,000 LY. (294 MLY)
NGC 7320 and all R = 6,700 km/s members is 59,000 LY. (354 MLY)
NGC 7318B and all R = 6,700 km/s members is 10,000 LY. (60 MLY)

Note: Traditional redshift separation is shown in brackets.

Summary

It is surely quite remarkable that galaxy associations, with such highly discordant redshifts, can be made to yield exceedingly plausible separations - *free of contradiction* - in the light of principles inherent in the "New Cosmology." And yet, this is but one example of a host of celestial anomalies which may be resolved upon the basis of a revised concept of radiation propagation and the premise of gravitational repulsion - including an explanation of our expanding universe without recourse to a Big Bang cosmology!

Once considered a full explanation for the phenomenon of gravitation, Newtonian mechanics is now seen to require modification by no less than three additional equations. By way of recapitulation, it may be stated that this enigmatic force must receive expression as follows:

THE ETERNAL UNIVERSE

1. The traditional Newtonian *inverse-square law.*
2. A so-called relativistic *adjustment for motion.* (In reality, this formula depicts the declining efficiency of gravitation with an increase in relative motion.)
3. The prescribed *distance/repulsion* (D/R) formula, in which a portion of exchanged energy is acknowledged to induce repulsion.
4. A *time-lapse* factor (for which exact calibration is pending), as no physical reaction can take place in zero time.

Noting that the D/R factor can account for expansion of the universe - at the very distance where gravitational attraction is disclosed to be ineffective in binding galaxies together - it is further observed that this same premise is capable of clarifying a variety of "missing mass" mysteries. Promising to solve mass discrepancy problems involving clusters of galaxies and galactic halos, this same D/R concept is also seen to afford a most logical explanation for perturbations detected in the orbits of the outer planets of our Solar System and in such binary star systems as DI Herculis. Clearly, it is much more than a coincidence that so many seemingly unrelated mysteries may be resolved by this one hitherto ignored principle of gravitational repulsion! Failure to concede that there is a repulsive side to gravitation, in view of overwhelming evidence to the contrary, can only serve to erode confidence in the scientific method.

Science seems to have a way of progressing in cycles, exhibiting periods of stagnation interspersed with sudden quantum leaps forward in response to new ideas and advanced technology. There is every reason to believe that conditions are now favorable to remedy misconceptions that have clouded such fundamental issues as gravitation, light propagation and cosmic origin. Hopefully, in assessing the many revolutionary implications of the "New Cosmology," the scientific community will not allow the instinctive prejudice of man to refute ideas simply because they require admission of past error.

Chapter 7

SCIENCE AND PHILOSOPHY

(The Great Cosmic Pyramid - The "Time Constant" of Spiritual Fusion - The Final Stages of Human Evolution.)

Both theoretical and observational evidence would appear to lend strong confirmation to the concept of a bound and finite physical universe. But many questions remain unanswered. Not the least of our problems is the need to devise a formula linking cosmic expansion with the *Motivation* behind creation. Furthermore, it must be conceded that the very existence of an enclosed system does not preclude the possibility of *other* universes! However, restricted as we are by limited insight, at our present stage of evolution, it is perhaps prudent to reserve comment to that which *is* conducive to investigation. In so doing, it will be shown that the physical cosmos is characterized by a rather unique series of mathematical relationships - a feature which would seem to indicate that, for all practical purposes, *our own universe must constitute a bound system sufficient unto itself!*

The Great Cosmic Pyramid

A most instructive picture of the universe emerges as a result of scientific deduction and logic. At the lower extremities of the Cosmic Pyramid the intrinsic worth or value of a particle of matter is revealed to be directly related to the quantity of "congealed energy" fused together into a common body - an entity that is as one with regard to such properties as space and time. Above the realm of atomic nuclei, with their enormously enhanced complexity and status in comparison to an elementary "A", we soon encounter a revolutionary stage of expression in the form of organic life.

This new level is characterized by a marked transformation, in the sense that fusion of larger quantities of "A" no longer serves to produce a corresponding increase in the mass of an entity! At this stage any further "desire" must be manifested in some other manner and upon an entirely higher plane. For instead of expending energy as gravitation, in a senseless endeavor to attract mere matter which now lies well below its status, such effort is directed to the task of achieving maximum interaction and harmony with similar members of its own world. Subsequently, as organic evolution progresses upward to the status of man at his pinnacle, so it may be inferred that these higher levels of spirit must represent fantastic amounts of energy since contained and converted to increased segments of God's Nature. A superior cosmic status, being the product of *deserved* spiritual fusion, may only be obtained with the passage of time and at the expense of a great deal of effort or energy, as we are often quite aware.

Even the strange paradox of Eternity begins to shed some of its aura of mystery, once the phenomenon of time receives interpretation as a relative experience - one that will surely vanish among members should interaction ever reach the point where it becomes instantaneous. To the extent that this ultimate degree of reciprocal communion is achieved, so there will no longer exist any reason for separate identities, and such components will henceforth lose their previous personalities and become united into fewer entities of greater worth. Time may thus be viewed as a unique attribute of *imperfection,* prevailing at all levels of creation below that of God, but having no substance or meaning once Perfection is reached - a state which might well be described as one of *Instantaneous Motion or Total Communion!* Eternity or Timelessness, rather than the transitory world of space and time, is disclosed to be the normal cosmic state! Just as surely as time appears at the lowest strata of creation, so it will cease to have any meaning at the apex of the Great Cosmic Pyramid once spirit is deserving of being united into One Harmonious Whole.

Viewed upon the large-scale, the rate by which spiritual fusion occurs throughout the universe cannot possibly be ascribed to a random factor. It is clearly a phenomenon in which advancement at one level is intimately connected with the progress achieved at all other levels! The equilibrium of the cosmos can only be maintained if spirit of the lowest caliber is created at a rate capable of balancing evolutionary movement to higher levels. Similarly, the frequency of fusion must facilitate a steady upward flow of spirit, free from the catastrophe of disruption that would arise should either a shortage or surplus be produced at any one level.

Notwithstanding this necessity to preserve overall stability it is important to realize that - upon a short-term basis - there is no ironclad rule insisting that actual instances of physical fusion must always take place, over the entire range of cosmic steps, with unswerving regularity. On the contrary, it is sufficient only that adjustments intercede periodically to restore long-term balance. Judging by the relative abundances of the many physical body-forms, housing a wide range of spiritual complexes, it is evident that phases of both literal fusion and quasi-fusion exist side by side in the universe.

Although a pattern of literal fusion (with an accompanying reduction of numbers) may be inferred during the evolution of "A" to the level of the fundamental particles of matter, a certain complexity surrounds the involvement of animate structures. A vast gap seems to prevail between the numbers of the material particles and elementary life forms. This wide discrepancy must surely indicate that, upon occasion, a great many spiritual entities may undergo delayed fusion into one radically different and higher structure! Prior to this significant event, justification could be rendered in a quasi-fusion state. In a sense, spirit may enjoy the "fruits of fusion" without a literal fusion having been effected. At the "pre-life" stage this condition is probably fulfilled within the extremely hot and dense interiors of stars, especially degenerate stars where reciprocal communion must be so magnified as to simulate actual fusion.

The course of biological life appears to be characterized by a mixture of fusion and quasi-fusion. In addition to a reduction of body-forms with status there are also instances where the advantages of fusion - without fusion - are readily available, in varying degrees, to many life forms. Man, for example, affords an excellent illustration of the benefits accruing from the ability to commune with other members of one's species. By reason of this opportunity to cooperate and share a wealth of knowledge and experiences his environmental status is seen to be enhanced to an extent not otherwise possible.

This leads us to ponder the long-term prospectus of mankind as a physical entity. Quite regardless of any inferred future reduction of population with evolutionary progress, it is inevitable that man's present quasi-fusion era must continue to alleviate instances of any spiritual injustice until his planet's final demise. What, then? Indeed, since it is rather inconceivable that man as such could ever expect to conclude his evolution toward Perfection without there most assuredly being some transitional stage, we may well ask the nature of this new and highly revolutionary structural form.

Strangely enough, his destiny could very conceivably be found in the stars! If this should seem slightly melodramatic we have merely to consider the unique properties of fully degenerate stars - stupendous concentrations of matter so compressed as to virtually constitute *super atomic particles!* Not only can we point to the incredible density of a neutron star (about half a million Earths compacted into a sphere only 20 miles or so in diameter), but the stellar black hole state of matter may be described as a total collapse and absolute fusion of a slightly greater segment of creation.

Becoming manifest as a spiritual entity of tremendous worth, once a critical stage of contraction is achieved, yet another quasi-fusion era may be initiated as a star of superdense proportions continues its development upon a new plane of existence. One can only speculate as to the details involved in subsequent evolution. Presumably, progress is facilitated by means of establishing reciprocal communion with similar entities - *interaction of a non-physical nature and not restricted to the velocity of light!* Finally, upon attaining the ability to express Total or instantaneous Communion, time will cease to exist for such advanced entities and *a literal fusion into God will ensue!* Somehow, as a consequence of *black holes* concluding this momentous transition from the physical world of imperfection and time, the surplus "energy" so released is manifested as a new generation of "A" within the confines of the Cosmic Creation Zone!

By way of illustrating the close interrelationship of cosmic extremes we might point to five rather curious numerical associations embracing phenomena of the ultra-small and the ultra-large. Involving the immense sum of 10^{40} (1 followed by 40 zeros), these similarities may be stated as follows:

(1) At really close proximity the electrical charge of a positive/negative pair of particles exceeds their mutual gravitational influence by a factor of very nearly 10^{40}.

(2) The density ratio of highly degenerate stars, as compared with the average density of matter throughout the expanse of the universe, is of the order of 10^{40}.

(3) Stretched out in a straight line, like a string of beads, it would take about 10^{40} proton nuclei to reach the distance at

which the galaxies are receding at the speed of light.

(4) The repulsive aspect of gravitation, at a distance equal to the diameter of a "maximum" particle nucleus, is seen to be some 10^{20} times weaker than attraction - in essence, such repulsion is the square root of attraction.

(5) The square root of the number of protons within our "observable universe" (10^{80}), is none other than 10^{40}.

In each instance these relationships may apparently be looked upon as an expression of *fusion versus non-fusion.* Not only do they tend to substantiate the underlying cosmic principle of fusion, but there is even reason to suspect that *a valuable clue lies therein as to the number of "A"s fused within the level of a "maximum" particle of matter!*

It will be recalled that gravitational influence, in the last analysis, had to be defined as an inborn desire for fusion on the part of all material components of creation - a universal expression of intrinsic worth expressed over the depths of outer space. Essentially, it is a reflection of a particle's ability to achieve attraction or communion with the physical *universe as a whole.* By contrast, the electrical force of a particle is a manifestation of this same worth condensed to a volume of space equal to that of its *immediate self:* the halo of energy surrounding the material body in question. Since there is good reason to believe that the value of "A" fused within a proton or an electron does not exceed that of the halo by an exorbitant figure, it follows that exposure to another charged particle will produce a magnified reaction *that is largely in proportion to the quantity of "A" involved!* Hence, it is to be inferred that roughly 10^{40} "A"s likely constitute a "maximum" particle! In a sense, the electrical force may be considered an indication of *achieved* fusion; whereas gravitation may be viewed as a sign of *potential* fusion associated with Destiny.

With regard to the second similarity, a fully degenerate star must represent a state of intimate communion tantamount to "maximum" density or fusion into one overall entity. On the other hand, the average density of matter in space may be defined as the "minimum" degree of interaction that is permitted to exist without requiring new creation. Within the Cosmic Creation Zone the introduction of "A" will be inferred in regions falling below average density, in contrast to those forms achieving critical condensation leading to a degree of Total Fusion. In essence, these extremes may be thought of as depicting maximum and minimum concentrations of energy within the framework of a bound system - one in which the velocity of light denotes total separation.

The connection between the diameter of a proton nucleus and the size of our universe is, of course, directly linked to the issue of average density and hydrogen abundance. Starting with the "maximum" fused state of a single proton, it will be seen that this overall distribution is consistent with a twofold increase in distance (and an eightfold increase in volume) for each fourfold increase in the number of such particles. Restated slightly, the pattern is one of a fourfold decrease in cosmic density with each doubling in the quantity of matter residing within the universe. To extend the picture, it is noted that a fourfold increase in mass is capable of expressing the same strength of gravitational influence over eight times the volume of space. On the surface this is possibly surprising, since it might be wondered why the two should not coincide. What mysterious factor enables gravitation to permeate as much space as it does?

The explanation presumably hinges upon a proper assessment of the roles played by time and evolutionary processes. For every increase in the creation of matter, so must it add to the task of achieving full communion in a universe where interaction among material structures is regulated by the velocity of light. Should we proceed upon the premise that every level of spirit is able to double its status in unit time, it may be deduced that each successive level must possess the power to attract twice the volume of "A". But since a larger amount of matter must lengthen the time required to unite creation, such an addition can only take the form of increased distance or separation - essentially, a disguised aspect of time or imperfection. The ensuing pattern of isolation, which would preserve equilibrium by fulfilling the basic requirement of each "A" being able to obtain fusion with another "A" in the same interval of time, is one of a fourfold increase in matter with every doubling of distance. Upon this basis a twofold decrease of density - beyond what would be expected to characterize a simple doubling in the quantity of matter - will be seen to accompany each "step" in the Cosmic Pyramid. For not only must spirit be unsatisfied to maintain the status quo, but it is motivated to seek its Ultimate Destiny through further fusion. Hence, in pondering the ability of gravitation to spread its influence over space, we are very likely witnessing a graphic demonstration of spirit striving unceasingly to effect a *future* doubling of status.

A philosophical basis for the inferred D/R factor would thus seem implicit in theory. It is surely more than a coincidence that, at the point where this subatomic repulsive force first becomes manifest, it does so as the square root of the number of fused "A"s which are believed to constitute the level of a "maximum" elementary particle! Indeed, it is essential that a twofold increase in the strength of extragalactic repulsion induce a fourfold increase of distance in order to achieve a balance between the rate of new creation and the rate of cosmic evolution. *In effect, it is the rate of spiritual advancement which determines the time scale of Hubble's constant!*

With a total of 10^{80} protons comprising our physical universe, and 10^{40} fused "A"s per proton, it will be inferred that Perfection - or any one "level" within the Great Cosmic Pyramid - is equivalent to some 10^{120} "A"s. In terms of spiritual evolution *this Ultimate State would involve approximately 400 "steps," or occasions of doubling.* Subsequently, an entity of the status of a proton is acknowledged to reside 1/3rd of the way toward the top of the Pyramid, having already climbed some 133 "steps" from its origin as an infinitesimal "A". Upon this premise, slightly less than one percent of all the mass-energy in the universe is likely to be incorporated into actual "maximum" particles.

Such an assumption can be put to a rather interesting test. What may prove to be so highly significant about this figure is the excellent agreement with certain cosmological considerations as they pertain to the Steady-state model of creation. According to this principle there are very definite limitations as to the relationship between average total density and the rate of cosmic expansion. With Hubble's constant established at roughly 12 billion years, no more than a few percent of all the material in the universe may be concentrated in the form of galaxies without threatening stability. Were a substantial proportion locked up inside stars it would contradict the assumption of continuous creation, which demands a preponderance of newly created matter forms between the clusters of exterior systems. Conversely, too great an abundance in the depths of space, with Hubble's constant being what it is, could lead to the spectacle of our gravitationally weak Local Group of galaxies possessing a lower than average density - thereby causing the cluster to expand apart, which it is obviously not doing. On the whole, our inferred ratio of mass-energy to actual matter, within the expanse of the universe, is seen to afford a most remarkable agreement with observation!

The "Time Constant" of Spiritual Fusion

Certainly a most intriguing prospect now awaiting us is that of determining the universal *"time constant,"* which must surely regulate the entire process of spiritual fusion. For it is an integral feature of theory that all levels of spirit, within the Great Cosmic Pyramid, must succeed in doubling their worth in some common interval of time. A solution to this problem will make it possible to derive a useful picture as to the average time that an individual must serve in order to achieve the equivalent of one doubling of status. Moreover, it will also provide insight into the highly relevant question as to when one may expect a future rebirth!

Evaluation of this time aspect entails consideration of certain factors. For instance, the rate of disintegration (at the edge of the universe) must be included in any equation attempting to express events in terms of a human lifetime. Due to the steady annihilation of worlds containing various life forms there will prevail a situation in which disrupted levels of spirit are compelled to seek rebirth on appropriate planets still residing within the Cosmic Creation Zone. Along with other factors pointing toward a similar conclusion, this introduces the suspicion that, in terms of the planet with which a spirit was last associated, considerable time could elapse between reincarnations. In other words, biological evolution is likely to reflect a "sharing" of available body-forms with displaced spirit from alien worlds - with the result that spiritual entities are, in effect, excused from having a physical manifestation over most of the course of a planet's lengthy history! (Time, of course, simply does not exist to spirit between incarnations, just as it appears to cease when we fall into a deep and dreamless sleep.)

Thus, in theory, it could follow that those who manage to increase their intrinsic worth in excess of the average will receive what might well be equivalent to a longer postponement in their next rebirth - thereby enhancing the likelihood of securing an existence in more suitable surroundings. On the other hand, one who has made relatively little or no progress (whether or not restricted by premature death) may expect to be reborn in but a

THE ETERNAL UNIVERSE

fraction of this time and, if so justified, in a less favorable environment should a regression be involved. Perhaps, in this manner, nature permits us some latitude in determining the circumstances into which we are reborn - including the specific moment of rebirth within an evolutionary era! Most assuredly, there is a great advantage to be gained from being reincarnated in a more advanced and civilized age.

No greater enigma confronts the inquisitive mind of mortal man than the challenge raised by the *"time constant"* of spiritual fusion. For without a steady and orderly upward flow of spirit, toward an Ultimate State of Perfection at the apex of the Cosmic Pyramid, the universe would be totally lacking in both Purpose and Justice. In spite of the many uncertainties that must be encountered when pioneering into virgin territory, a solution of the time/evolution relationship is a task which cannot be avoided if true knowledge is to be our goal. While admittedly posing a structure of high complexity, our present-day universe is not without numerous clues and much vital information - information that would have been richly treasured by many wise scientists and philosophers of the past! If complete success is not to be within our immediate grasp, it should never be because we lack the fortitude to try.

Clearly, the *rate of expansion* of the universe must constitute a key factor in any approach to the time aspect of cosmic evolution. Why does the universe double its size in an interval of some 12 billion years? Why this particular figure? Obviously, the greater the rate of expansion the greater the degree of disintegration at the edge of the universe. Inasmuch as this disintegration factor must be balanced through creation, it will be seen that the introduction and evolution of new "A" is closely related to the recession of the galaxies. The issue, therefore, is basically one of determining precisely how "A" is introduced with respect to each cycle of Hubble's constant.

Upon due consideration, the one logical possibility to emerge would seem to embrace the premise that *one entire level of new "A" is created in just such a span of time, and is able to fulfill its Destiny by evolving to a state of Perfection in this same interval!* Should this be the case it must follow that the time required by spirit, to double its worth, may be determined by dividing Hubble's constant by the number of "steps" or doublings separating "A" from Perfection.

THE ETERNAL UNIVERSE

Assuming a proton to consist of 10^{40} "A"s, and a physical universe of 10^{80} protons, we have a spiritual pyramid of some 10^{120} "A"s per level and a total of approximately 400 "steps." (In view of the most unique relationship of the sum of 10^{40}, as it relates to the size of our finite universe, along with the inability of material forms to communicate at velocities exceeding that of light, it is perhaps in order to treat such a region as though it constituted a complete system terminating in what - for all practical purposes - we may describe as God.) Subsequently, a period of roughly 30 million years per occasion of doubling may be derived.

Proceeding upon this basis, it will be deduced that only 1/400th of an entire level of new "A" will be created in a period of 30 million years. In effect, this means that only one spiritual entity in 400 may have a "conscious" (or physical) manifestation at any given instant! But if 30 million years is the allotted time, in which one *entire* level of spirit must double its status, this restriction will introduce an additional factor of 400 into the time permitted for actual instances of physical incarnation. Dividing our 30 million year period by this further factor of 400, we are left with about 75,000 years as the average elapsed time for a "conscious" existence between doublings.

Yet another factor is imposed by disintegration at the edge of the universe, as displaced spirit must periodically be reborn within the confines of the Cosmic Creation Zone. Since it takes time for new stars and planets to form and evolve biological entities, it is evident that this factor is very much related to status. Calculation of the average age of matter, within the framework of the Steady-state model, yields the information that only about one part in 20 will be as old as Hubble's constant.

Upon this line of reasoning the average time required by spirit - as a "conscious" entity - to double in value may be expressed by the formula:

$$T = \frac{SH}{DLS^2} \qquad \text{or:} \qquad T = \frac{H}{DLS}$$

THE ETERNAL UNIVERSE

Where:

T = Time required to achieve one doubling of status in terms of a "conscious" existence.

S = Total number of cosmic "steps" from "A" to Perfection (or Full Communion) within a finite physical universe some 18 BLY in radius.

H = Hubble's constant (deduced to be about 12 BY).

D = Disintegration factor at the edge of the universe in one cycle of Hubble's constant.

L = Level of spirit in question - defined in terms of the number of "steps" evolved beyond the initial state of "A".

Assuming that 400 "steps" extend between "A" and Total Communion, it now becomes essential to determine the position of mankind in this overall scheme. With a hydrogen atom established at "step" 133, this problem may well be resolved by a comparison of the relative abundance of the proton to man throughout the Cosmic Creation Zone.

By way of assessing this ratio it may be estimated that about 10^{22} Earth-type planets presently exist in the universe, of which only about one in 10^5 will currently feature biological evolution equivalent to man at his present level. Multiplying our estimated 10^{17} planets by the sum of 10^{10} (representing an average long-term population of man per planet), we arrive at a total of 10^{27} human beings at this particular level. Since some 10^{80} protons constitute our physical universe, we may deduce a ratio of about 10^{53} protons for every man. Translated into "steps" in the Cosmic Pyramid this sum is equal to some 177 doublings. Accordingly, the level of man may be derived by adding these 177 "steps" to the 133 "steps" believed to characterize a proton - leading to the conclusion that man presently resides at about the 310th "step."

With this information we may now attempt to resolve the "time constant" for man as per our formula. Therefore:

$$T = \frac{12{,}000{,}000{,}000}{20 \times 310 \times 400} = 4{,}800 \text{ years (approximately)}$$

Thus it would be calculated that, upon the average, man must serve a total of something like 4,800 years (or almost 70 lifetimes of 70 years) in order to double his intrinsic worth. (Any uncertainty in computing the ratio of man to proton will not seriously alter our estimate, since an error by a factor of a million will only make a difference of about 6%, and a million million by only 12%!)

With insight into man's status in the Cosmic Pyramid, along with knowledge of the "time constant" of spiritual fusion, we may now face the issue of reincarnation in terms of Earth evolution. During what past age did we last live? Moreover, in what future era are we likely to be reborn?

Considering the necessity of accommodating displaced spirit from other worlds, along with the overall cycle of doubling which is of the order of 30 million years, reincarnation may essentially take the form of a projection well into the future and into another planetary environment! Thus, if man requires 4,800 years as a "conscious" existence to achieve one doubling of status over a period of 30 million years, it will be tantamount to an elapsed time of almost 6,200 years for each year of a past life. Based upon an average life expectancy of 70 years this would call for a rebirth some four to five hundred thousand years into the future. However, if only 1/400th of an entire level of "A" is created per 30 million year cycle, in terms of Earth evolution the *apparent* elapsed time will be less than the *actual* time by this very same factor! Subsequently, for all intents and purposes, the reincarnation of man may be linked to the basic formula:

$$R = \frac{YH}{TS^2}$$

The two additional symbols may be defined as follows:
R = Rebirth of man (in years) in terms of a future era on Earth.
Y = The number of years lived during last incarnation.

Hence: $R = \dfrac{70 \times 12{,}000{,}000{,}000}{4{,}800 \times 400 \times 400} = 1{,}100$ years (approximately)

In other words, what probably transpires is that man is actually reborn some hundreds of thousands of years from now; but in relation to the environmental status with which he was last associated it will be equivalent to an evolutionary era only a thousand years or so into the future!

THE ETERNAL UNIVERSE

The Final Stages of Human Evolution

Upon contemplating the future of mankind, as a biological species, it may be theorized that each additional doubling will require some 75,000 years in terms of Earth evolution. The eventual passage of man, beyond his present transitory and rather frail human form, could very well have a solution in such an astronomical curiosity as a *celestial black hole!* Best described as an immense concentration of mass-energy contracted into virtual spatial oblivion, the ratio of mankind to this unique state of totally fused matter should permit computation of the number of "steps" needed to achieve this inferred evolution. With such being the case, it may indeed be said that man's destiny is to be found in the stars!

Strange as it might first appear, there are some very convincing arguments for linking man's future to a phenomenon that is almost so bizarre as to be mind-boggling. Not only does this state of "maximum" density express all the required attributes of complete fusion - thereby constituting a spiritual entity of a specific level - but an excellent agreement of numbers can be derived which would connect theory with observation. It is surely more than a remarkable coincidence that an estimate, of all the stellar black holes likely to exist in the universe, should turn out to be equal to the probable number of Earth-type planets that are allowed to fulfill their evolutionary roles. Moreover, it can be shown that the quantity of "A" fused within a typical stellar black hole (some 10^{58} protons x 10^{40} "A"s, or about 10^{98} fused "A"s), when multiplied by the number of such objects in the entire universe, is very likely of the same order as the total spiritual worth (or "A" content) of one complete population of Earth-man multiplied by the quantity of all other worlds of a similar evolutionary level. The implication is little short of obvious: *A stellar black hole may well represent the eventual destiny of a humanity, so deserving of intimate harmony, as to become fused into a new entity of truly enormous magnitude!*

By way of determining the number of cosmic "steps," between present man and the exalted status of a stellar black hole, it is necessary to examine what transpires as man finally evolves beyond his current level which we might define as M^1. Upon doubling his worth, and attaining the status of M^2, it will be noted that a gap has suddenly appeared in our planet's otherwise unbroken chain of evolutionary life forms. In effect, there is no longer an M^1 level. Similarly, after M^2 progresses to the status of M^3, the gap will widen to include the absence of both M^1 and M^2 levels. For the first time in our planet's history *a gap has occurred in the evolutionary continuum* - one that will grow steadily in size until man's eventual extinction as a biological entity! Assuming that only about one Earth-type planet in 10^5 will feature human life equivalent to a specific "M" level, it may be deduced that some 17 doublings will suffice to accomplish the inferred evolution from M^1 to the status of a stellar black hole. Accordingly, this momentous stage may be looked upon as constituting "step" number 327 in a Cosmic Pyramid of 400 "steps."

The hidden significance of this 17 "step" gap, in the evolutionary sequence of all Earth-type planets, lies in its ability to resolve a paradox with regard to a final merger of spirit into a stellar black hole. Without the existence of this gap, which must result in stellar black holes outnumbering any one specific "M" level by a factor of 10^5, we would encounter a somewhat outlandish situation at the more advanced stages of man's evolution. Since theory demands a reduction of numbers in direct proportion to higher status, it follows that the final "M" stages would otherwise be quite literally populated by a mere handful of individuals. The inferred gap of some 17 "steps" will greatly alleviate this problem by assuring that the ultimate "M" stage, immediately prior to achieving stellar black hole fusion, will consist of not less than 10^5 spiritual entities. When combined with the ratio of 10^5 stellar black holes in excess of a solitary "M" stage, we arrive at a total of 10^{10} entities - exactly the sum needed to account for a typical M^1 population level! No wonder there is a curious similarity in the numbers of stellar black holes and Earth-type planets! It does, in fact, seem to necessitate an apparent "surplus" of 10^5 stellar black holes in order to balance cosmic books in terms of "A" content.

To grasp the full picture of this crucial relationship, involving relative abundance and fused "A" content of the various cosmic levels, it is perhaps constructive to assess the total range of "M" stages in some detail. (See Appendix #4.) Immediately prior to our present M^1 stage, it will be noted, the abrupt increase (10^5) in worlds must require a corresponding reduction in the number of pre-human entities. This is precisely what is observed when we examine the distribution of our own terrestrial life forms. The comparative shortage of primitive man is clearly no accident; nor is the recent sharp increase in human population an unprecedented occurrence. In both instances we are likely witnessing nature's balancing of appropriate cosmic equations. (Incidently, the relative scarcity of early man tends to substantiate the conclusion that there is really little difference in spiritual value between the higher animals and primitive man - with the family pet possibly only short steps away in the evolutionary ladder!)

In predicting the future of mankind, as he passes through successive "M" levels, it is to be inferred that each doubling will involve about 75,000 years in terms of Earth history. After all 17 "M" levels (or generations of human doubling) have been attained, it may be calculated that some 1,275,000 years will have elapsed as mankind finally concludes his evolutionary saga on the planet Earth. From this point onward our world will continue to feature all present life forms below that of M^1; but any trace of a higher intelligence will likely be conspicuous by its absence. In actuality, *man will have vanished from the face of this planet simply because he succeeded in evolving beyond the human form!* (This deduction would readily explain any difficulty in contacting intelligent life forms on other planets. It is not so much that they are intrinsically scarce in our Galaxy, as it is that large numbers of such civilizations have already come and gone in the relatively short time span allocated for human supremacy!)

Invariably, it is the evolution of the human brain itself which provides the mechanism for his eventual reduction of numbers. Along with the degree of spiritual progress achieved during a past life, the rebirth of a soul must be regulated by two basic factors. On the one hand we have the quantity of spirit awaiting incarnation; while on the other we have the number of suitable body-forms available for housing a specific level of spirit. With evolution serving to gradually change the structure and caliber of man's brain, the incorporation of human souls will become highly restrictive as fewer entities of a particular status seek manifestation in fewer appropriate body-forms. Essentially, nature will be seen to impose its own foolproof method of birth control. As man pursues his ascent of the Cosmic Pyramid, so the emphasis will be shifted from quantity to quality. (See Figure #12.)

Beyond the lofty status of a stellar black hole lies another universe embracing new and unfamiliar laws. Within this world of

THE ETERNAL UNIVERSE

Principle spirit is enabled to climax its lengthy evolution by transcending such mundane attributes as time, electricity and gravitational interaction. In the eyes of mortal man the black hole state must be worshiped as a wondrous God-like realm of reciprocal communion - from whence Perfection will ultimately ensue as Total Fusion of Black Hole Minds becomes a reality and time ceases to exist! Somehow, as a direct consequence of this momentous transition from a world of imperfection and time, the mass-energy so released is manifested as a new generation of "A" within the confines of our physical universe.

Perhaps, of all matter forms subject to instant disintegration at the edge of the universe, the unique properties of black holes could suffice to preserve them from sharing the same abrupt fate. Such an exception might even turn out to be both a logical and a necessary inference - especially in the case of the more massive quasar-type black holes. Ranging in size from several solar masses, for a typical stellar black hole, it is conceivable that an unbroken chain of singularities could prevail up to some billions of times the mass of our Sun. If the supermassive black hole at the center of the giant galaxy M87 (about 5 billion solar masses) is any indication, this would seem to represent the upper limit for the size of a black hole. Calculation of the "A" content, for an object of this nature, leads to a total of something like 10^{108} fused "A"s. For an entity of this evolutionary status its theoretical abundance appears to be much higher than what is observed. This discrepancy is effectively removed, however, by the simple expedient of exempting black holes - at least supermassive quasar-type entities - from any premature extinction at the cosmic periphery.

In any event, a truly amazing picture emerges as to what lies beyond the human form. We are at last in a position to glimpse a future that must exceed our wildest dreams. Upon contemplating the premise of an Eternal Universe, it may well be said that mankind now stands at the threshold of an entirely new and promising field of inquiry, the surface of which has barely been scratched. The challenge to man is clearly without parallel; but the reward will far more than justify his efforts!

THE ETERNAL UNIVERSE

ERA	PERIOD		EPOCH	LIFE	YEARS AGO (MILLIONS)
CENOZOIC	QUATERNARY		RECENT	PRIMITIVE MAN	2 +
			PLEISTOCENE		
	TERTIARY		PLIOCENE	EARLY PRIMATES	12
			MIOCENE		26
			OLIGOCENE	MAMMALS	38
			EOCENE	HAVE REPLACED	54
			PALEOCENE	DINOSAURS	65
MESOZOIC	CRETACEOUS			FLOWERING PLANTS	136
	JURASSIC			PRIMITIVE BIRDS AND MAMMALS	195
	TRIASSIC			DINOSAURS	225
PALEOZOIC	PERMIAN			REPTILES	280
	CARBON-IFEROUS	PENNSYLVANIAN		INSECTS	320
		MISSISSIPPIAN		LUSH FORESTS	
	DEVONIAN			AMPHIBIANS	345
	SILURIAN			LAND FERNS	395
	ORDOVICIAN			MANY FISHES	430
	CAMBRIAN			TRILOBITES	500
				MARINE LIFE	570
PRECAMBRIAN				INVERTEBRATES SIMPLE CELLS ELEMENTARY LIFE FORMS	700
					3,500 +

Fig. #1. DIVISIONS OF GEOLOGICAL TIME

Fig. #2

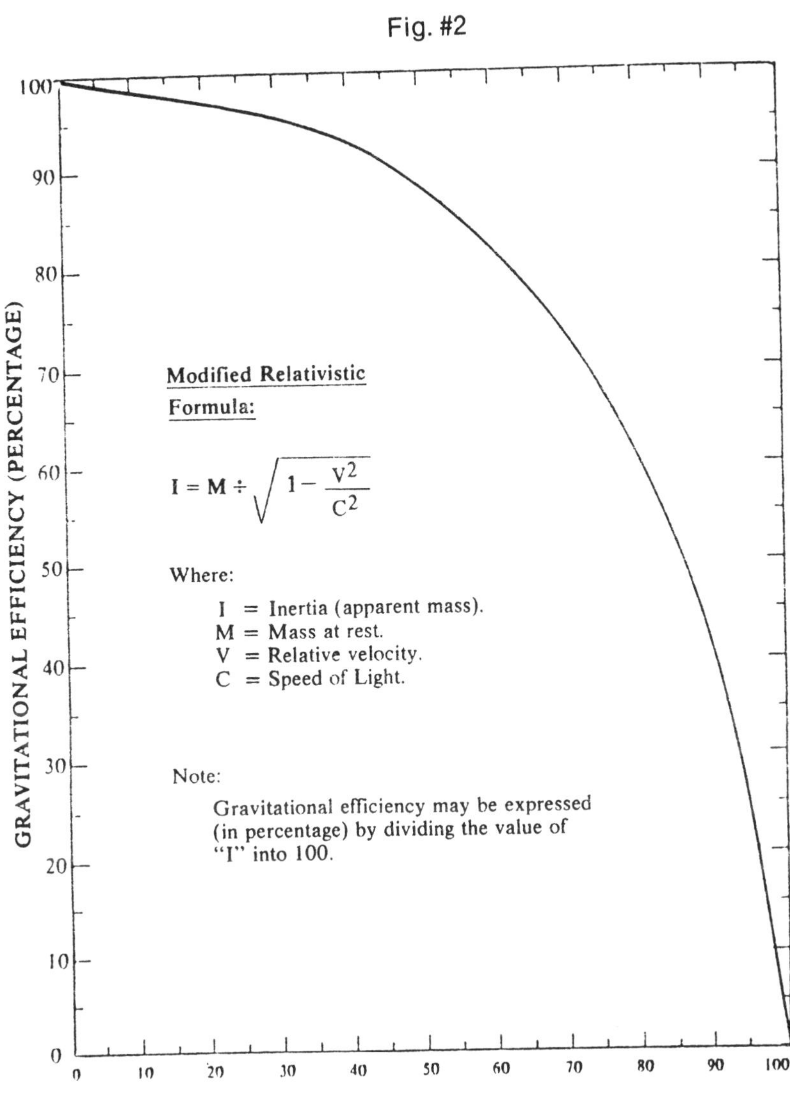

$$I = M \div \sqrt{1 - \frac{V^2}{C^2}}$$

EFFICIENCY OF GRAVITATION WITH RELATIVE MOTION

THE ETERNAL UNIVERSE

Fig. #3. DISTANCE/REPULSION RELATIONSHIP OF GRAVITATION

DISTANCE	REPULSION	DISTANCE	REPULSION
4-Fold Increase (From Elementary Particle Nucleus) (cm - km - ly)	2-Fold Increase (In Terms of Gravitational Attraction)	4-Fold Increase (From Elementary Particle Nucleus) (cm - km - ly	2-Fold Increase (In Terms of Gravitational Attraction)
1.5×10^{-13} cm	10^{-20}	110.680 km	8.590×10^{-10}
6×10^{-13} cm	2×10^{-19}	442.722 km	1.718×10^{-9}
2.4×10^{-12} cm	4×10^{-19}	1,770.89 km	3.436×10^{-9}
9.6×10^{-12} cm	8×10^{-19}	7.083.55 km	6.872×10^{-9}
3.84×10^{-11} cm	1.6×10^{-18}	28,334.2 km	1.374×10^{-8}
1.536×10^{-10} cm	3.2×10^{-18}	113,337 km	2.749×10^{-8}
6.144×10^{-10} cm	6.4×10^{-18}	453,347 km	5.498×10^{-8}
2.458×10^{-9} cm	1.28×10^{-17}	1.813×10^{6} km	1.100×10^{-7}
9.830×10^{-9} cm	2.56×10^{-17}	7.254×10^{6} km	2.200×10^{-7}
3.932×10^{-8} cm	5.12×10^{-17}	2.901×10^{7} km	4.398×10^{-7}
1.573×10^{-7} cm	1.024×10^{-16}	1.161×10^{8} km	8.796×10^{-7}
6.291×10^{-7} cm	2.048×10^{-16}	4.642×10^{8} km	1.759×10^{-6}
2.517×10^{-6} cm	4.096×10^{-16}	1.857×10^{9} km	3.518×10^{-6}
1.007×10^{-5} cm	8.192×10^{-16}	7.428×10^{9} km	7.037×10^{-6}
4.027×10^{-5} cm	1.638×10^{-15}	2.971×10^{10} km	1.407×10^{-5}
1.611×10^{-4} cm	3.277×10^{-15}	1.188×10^{11} km	2.815×10^{-5}
6.442×10^{-4} cm	6.554×10^{-15}	4.754×10^{11} km	5.629×10^{-5}
2.577×10^{-4} cm	1.311×10^{-14}	1.901×10^{12} km	1.126×10^{-4}
.010308 cm	2.621×10^{-14}	7.606×10^{12} km	2.252×10^{-4}
.041232 cm	5.243×10^{-14}	3.215847 ly	4.504×10^{-4}
.164927 cm	1.049×10^{-13}	12.86339 ly	9.007×10^{-4}
.659707 cm	2.097×10^{-13}	51.45355 ly	1.801×10^{-3}
2.63883 cm	4.194×10^{-13}	205.8142 ly	3.603×10^{-3}
10.5553 cm	8.389×10^{-13}	823.2568 ly	7.206×10^{-3}
42.2212 cm	1.678×10^{-12}	3,293.03 ly	.01441
168.885 cm	3.355×10^{-12}	13,172.1 ly	.02882
675.540 cm	6.711×10^{-12}	52.688.4 ly	.05765
2,702.2 cm	1.342×10^{-11}	210,754 ly	.11529
10,809 cm	2.684×10^{-11}	843.015 ly	.23058
43,235 cm	5.369×10^{-11}	3,372.060 ly	.46117
1.72938 km	1.074×10^{-10}	13,488.239 ly	.92234
6.91753 km	2.147×10^{-10}	(16.900.000 ly)	(1.0000)
27.6701 km	4.295×10^{-10}		

NOTE: This simplified formula does not express the need for a limited degree of small-scale modification in the immediate vicinity of high concentrations of mass, as the total amount of exchanged energy is the product of both mass and distance. Nevertheless, it is likely to prove useful in describing a wide range of phenomena.

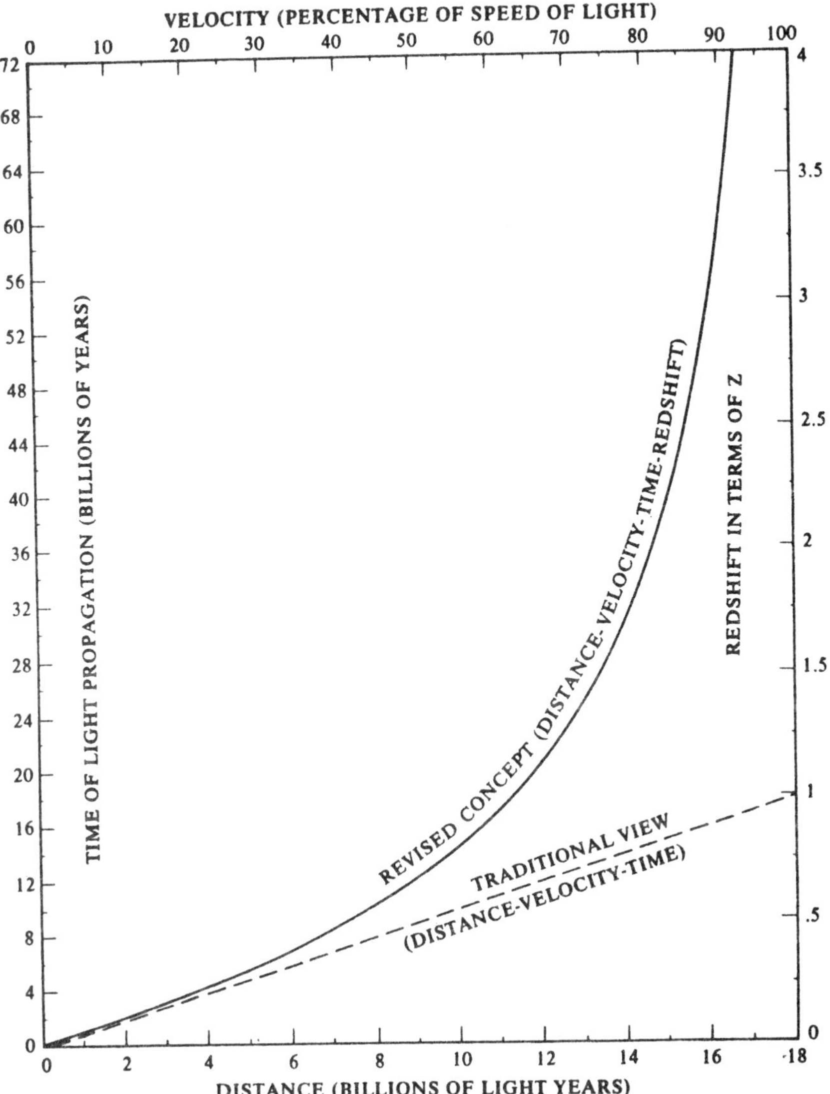

Fig. #4 (CONCENTRIC VIEW)
REDSHIFT/TIME/VELOCITY/DISTANCE SCALE

THE ETERNAL UNIVERSE

Fig. #5. EXPANSION OF UNIVERSE AND PROPAGATION OF LIGHT

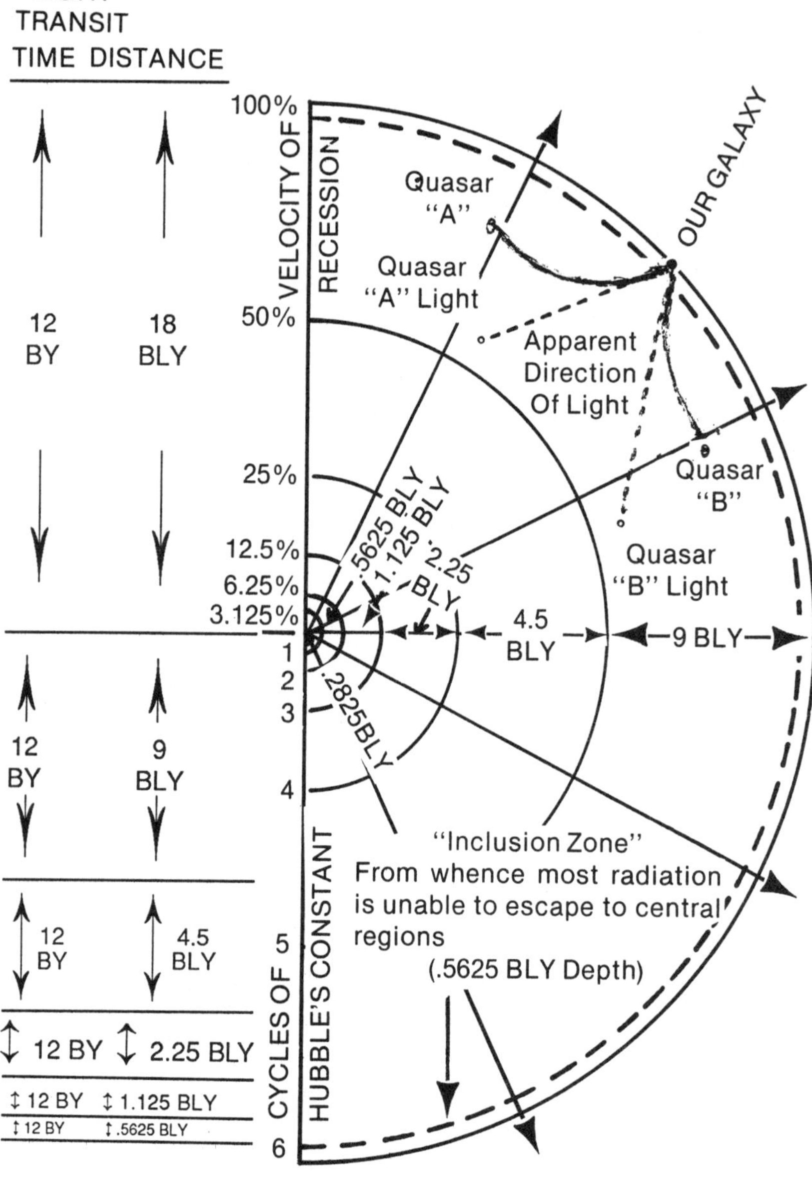

Fig. #6.

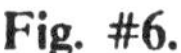

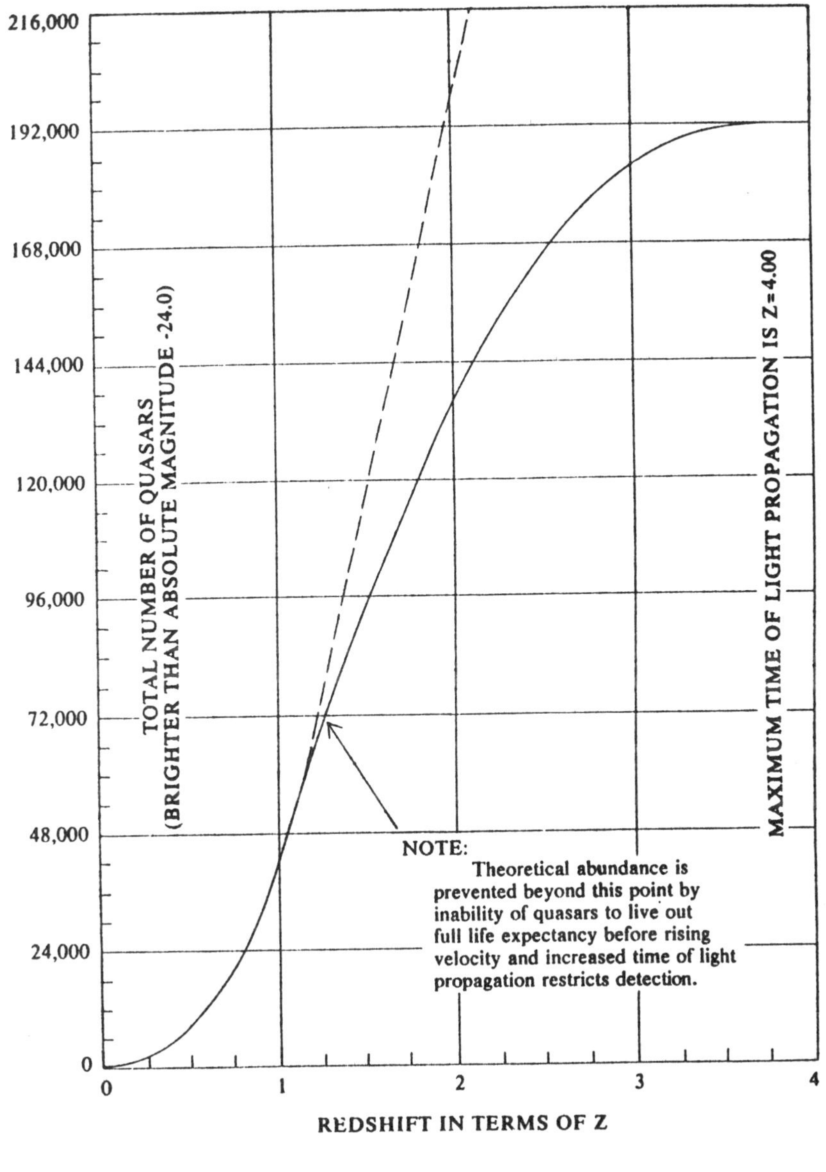

OBSERVABLE QUASARS IN TERMS OF Z REDSHIFT

THE ETERNAL UNIVERSE

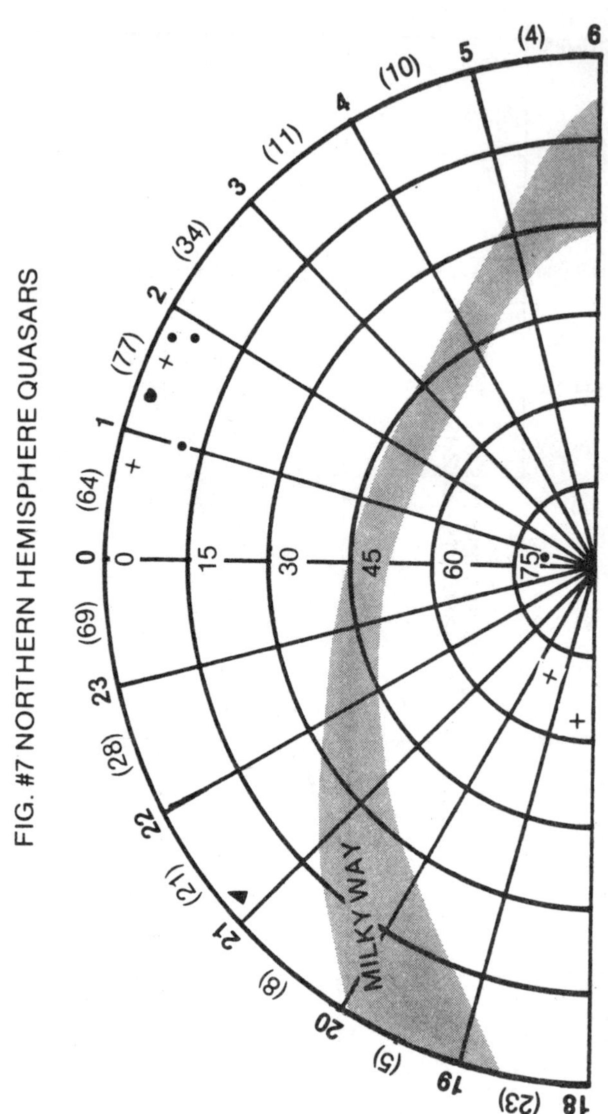

168

THE ETERNAL UNIVERSE

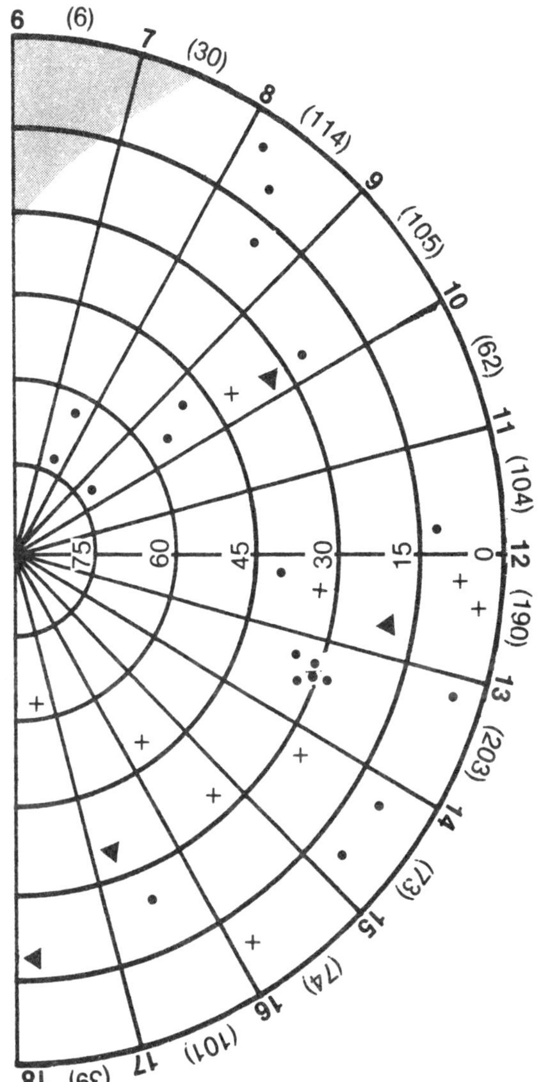

BRACKETED NUMBERS AT PERIPHERY GIVE TOTAL WITHIN CONICAL SEGMENT.

• - 29.0 AND UP (Z = 2.50 AND UP)
▲ - 27.0 AND UP (Z = .401 TO .600)
+ - 26.0 AND UP (UP TO Z = .400)

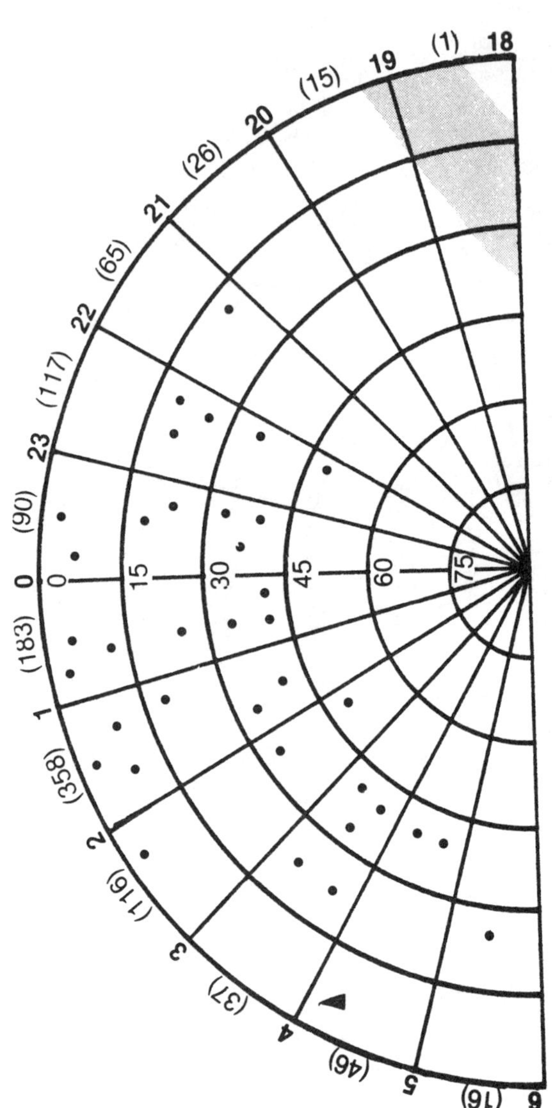
FIG. #8 SOUTHERN HEMISPHERE QUASARS
(1) 18
(15) 19
(26) 20
(65) 21
(117) 22
(90) 23
(183) 0
(358) 1
(116) 2
(37) 3
(46) 4
(16) 5
6
0
15
30
45
60
75

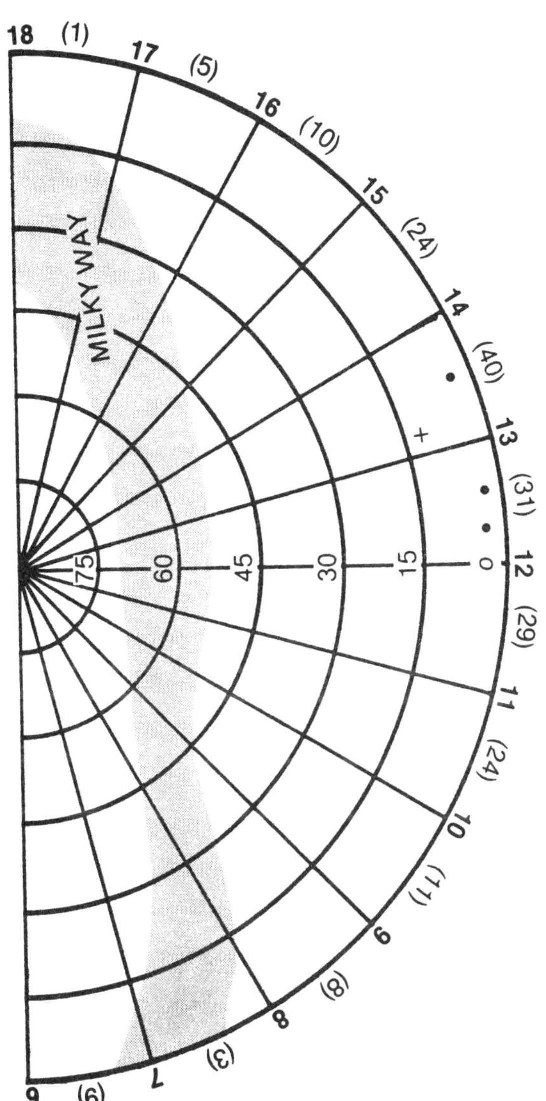
18
(1)
17
(5)
16
(10)
15
(24)
14
(40)
13
(31)
12
(29)
11
(24)
10
(11)
9
(8)
8
(3)
7
(6)
9
MILKY WAY
75
60
45
30
15
0
NOTE:
BRACKETED NUMBERS AT PERI-
PHERY GIVE TOTAL WITHIN CON-
ICAL SEGMENT.
• - 29.0 AND UP (Z = 2.50 AND UP)
▲ - 27.0 AND UP (Z = .401 TO .600)
+ - 26.0 AND UP (UP TO Z = .400)

THE ETERNAL UNIVERSE

MAGNITUDE DIFFERENCE

Redshift Range Z =	Average Magnitude (Difference per Bin)	Average Magnitude (Total Difference)	Quantity Edge	Balance
up to .200	* .0061	* .0061	22	60
.200 to .400	* .5572	* .3232	67	98
.400 to .600	* .2007	* .2458	67	103
.600 to .800	* .1688	* .2076	66	102
.800 to 1.00	* .3000	* .1788	71	90
1.00 to 1.20	* .1200	* .1715	60	94
1.20 to 1.40	* .1101	* .1959	61	109
1.40 to 1.60	* .0688	* .0887	96	100
1.60 to 1.80	* .2517	* .0689	91	102
1.80 to 2.00	# .3061	# .0645	140	145
2.00 to 2.20	# .2824	# .2275	212	144
2.20 to 2.40	# .1348	# .3061	206	106
2.40 to 2.60	# .4996	# .3108	50	59
2.60 to 2.80	# .8436	# .3316	38	36
2.80 to 3.00	# .5337	# .3482	29	22
over 3.00	# .8764	# .3696	39	35
			1,315	1,405

* = Brighter Away From Edge
\# = Brighter Toward Edge

Fig. #9. QUASAR LUMINOSITY BY REDSHIFT/DIRECTION

THE ETERNAL UNIVERSE

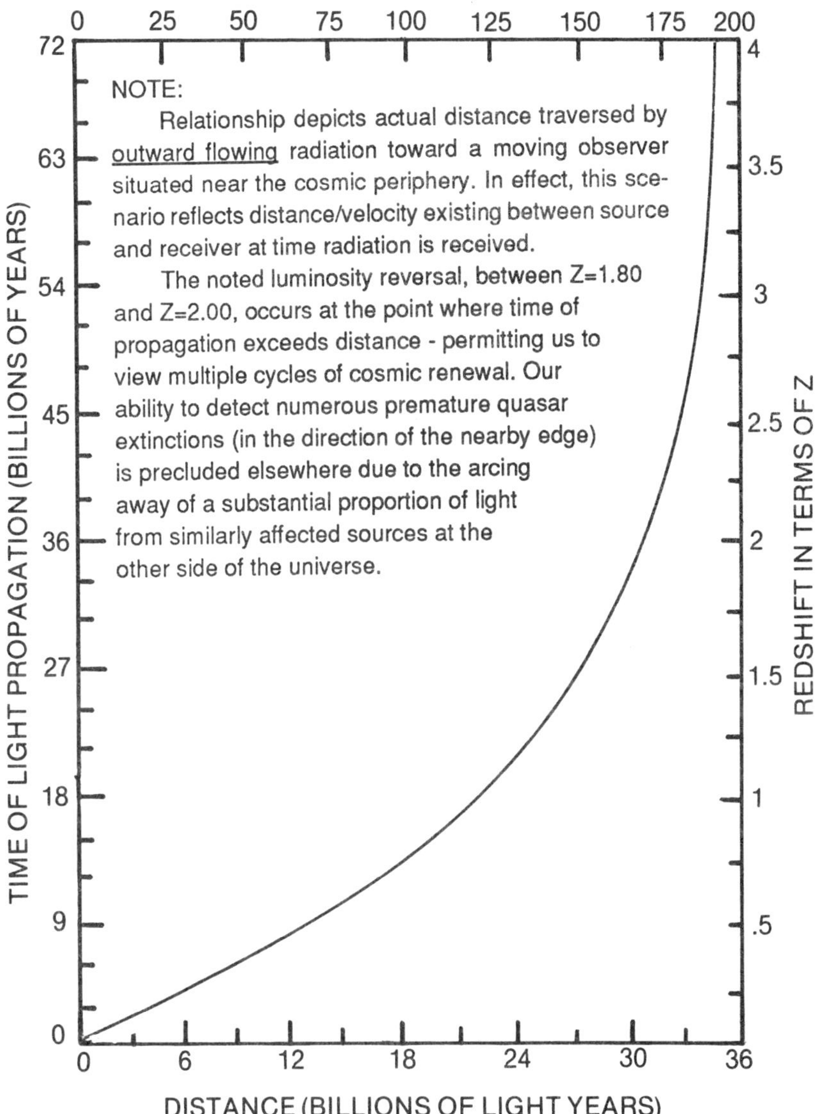

Fig. #10 (ECCENTRIC VIEW)
(REDSHIFT/TIME/VELOCITY/DISTANCE SCALE

THE ETERNAL UNIVERSE

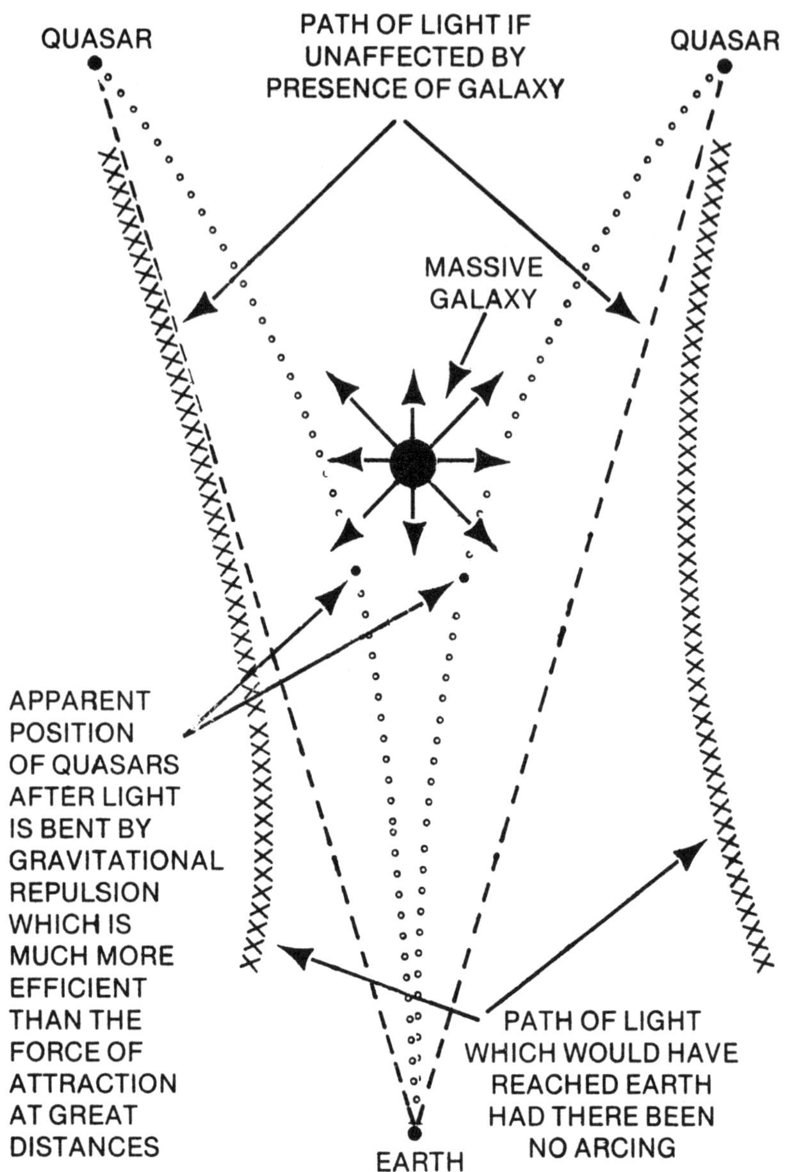

Fig. #11 GALACTIC ABERRATION OF RADIATION

THE ETERNAL UNIVERSE

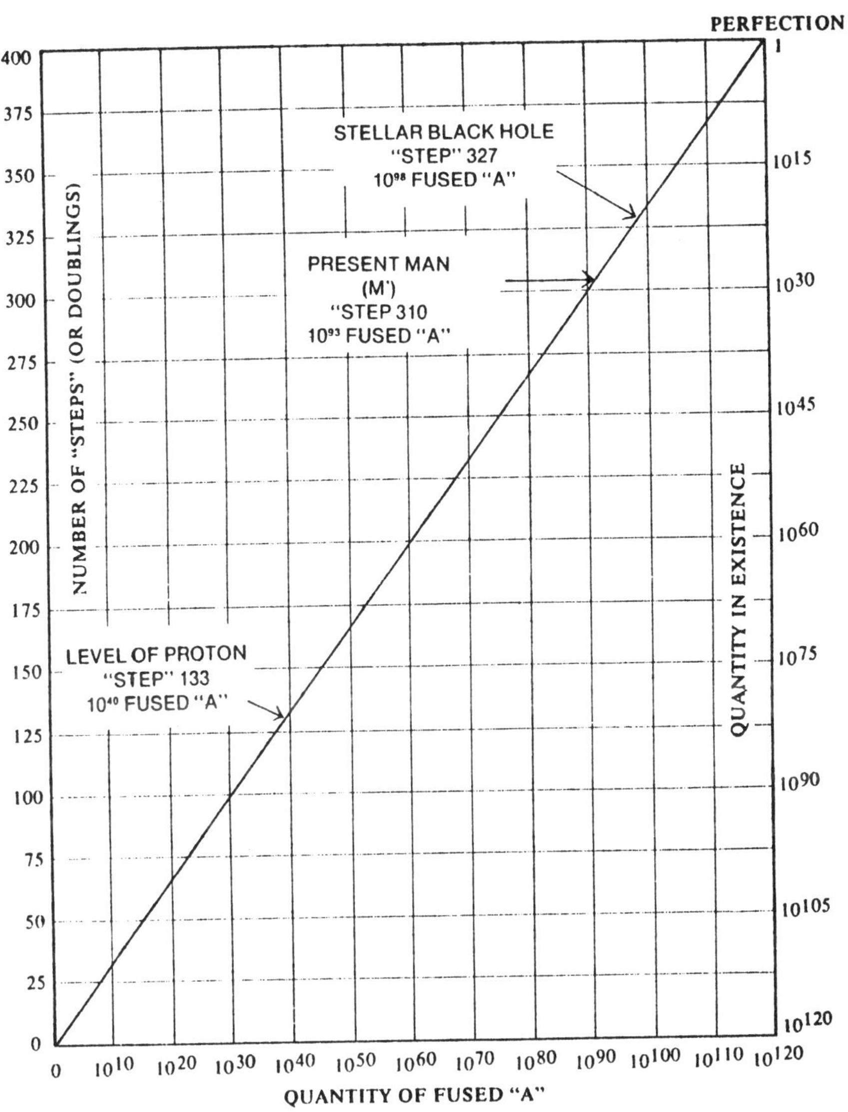

Fig. #12 PYRAMID STRUCTURE OF UNIVERSE

Appendix 1

Efficiency of Gravitation vs. Light Propagation

Velocity % of Light	Light Propagation Efficiency (%) $1+Z = \sqrt{\dfrac{C+V}{C-V}}$	Gravitational Efficiency (%) $I = M \div \sqrt{1-\dfrac{V^2}{C^2}}$	Excess Efficiency of Gravitation as Opposed to Light Propagation (%)
zero	100.000000	100.000000	zero
1	99.497537	99.994990	.49996
2	98.990298	99.979994	.99979
3	98.477537	99.954980	1.50028
4	97.960223	99.919964	2.00054
5	97.437586	99.874926	2.50143
10	94.749458	99.498745	5.01246
15	91.934353	98.868597	7.54260
20	88.989823	97.979582	10.10200
25	85.912306	96.824589	12.70165
30	82.696980	95.393923	15.35357
35	79.337500	93.674963	18.07148
40	75.825761	91.651518	20.87121
45	72.151437	89.302857	23.77141
50	68.301270	86.602543	26.79492
55	64.258236	83.516464	29.97005
60	60.000000	80.000000	33.33333
65	55.496714	75.993420	36.93318
70	50.707143	71.414283	40.83673
75	45.571891	66.143782	45.14162
80	40.000000	60.000000	50.00000
85	33.839135	52.678260	55.67259
90	26.794495	43.588980	62.67886
95	18.112495	31.224980	72.39469
96	16.000000	28.000000	75.00000
97	13.655245	24.310490	78.03041
98	10.949874	19.899740	81.73487
99	7.553368	14.106730	86.76078
99.9	2.285509	4.471010	95.62426
99.99	.712089	1.414210	98.60014
99.999	.224106	.447213	99.55405
99.9999	.070761	.141421	99.85881
99.99999	.022366	.044721	99.95573

Observation:

An instructive difference in efficiency is noted upon comparison of the two formulas — ranging from zero (at no relative motion) to a high of 100% at virtually the velocity of light — in which gravitation is seen to possess the greater efficiency.

Explanation:

The formula depicting gravitational efficiency does not take the expansion of the universe into consideration. In short, it fails to reflect *accelerating* velocity of recession; whereas the other formula does. The noted 100% maximum differential may be ascribed to impositions of time and distance. For instance, with an increase of recession velocity to that of light speed the factor of distance (equal to the radius of our universe) is introduced. However, since time is related to distance, it follows that any doubling of distance is equivalent to inducing a twofold increase in time of light propagation. Thus the subsequent discrepancy is seen to arise because the gravitational formula does not express light speed communion commensurate with enhanced distance imposed by cosmic expansion. In effect, this observation substantiates the view that gravitation is indeed propagated at the velocity of light — with efficiency very much dictated by relative motion!

Appendix 2

Multiple Radio Sources and Jets

Discovered more than a quarter of a century ago, radio galaxies continue to harbor unresolved mysteries. Typically, such an object may be described as an optical galaxy with extensive double radio lobes, emerging from opposing poles of the central star system, and stretching to distances of up to a million light years or more. Although these twin lobes have obviously been ejected from the polar regions of the parent galaxy, and while the presence of a supermassive rotating central black hole may well hold the key to an understanding (as many astronomers suspect), when it comes to details much clarification is still required. Proceeding upon the basis of reduced gravitational efficiency with increased relative motion, there is reason to believe that fresh insight into this curious phenomenon is now at hand.

Essentially, the energy source may be ascribed to infalling matter spiraling into the supermassive whirling black hole core of a radio galaxy. Due to extreme velocity of rotation, and acknowledging that the efficiency of gravitation is reduced dramatically as light speed is approached, an unusually large general influx of mass must lead to a bifurcated explosion. In effect, the rapid rotation of the black hole induces ingested matter to spiral inward from two preferred directions - namely, the opposed polar regions which will be seen to possess minimal rotational impetus that would act to divert and interfere with absorption. Broken down into relatively modest quanta through collision, overwhelming gravitational tides and an intense magnetic field, such infalling matter forms are accelerated to the velocity of light and expelled as radiation (of radio wavelengths) in the opposite polar direction from whence it is received!

The peculiar nature of somewhat less common single jets, which tend to be associated with more powerful galaxies and quasars, almost certainly has a related explanation. (M87, the supergiant elliptical galaxy at the very heart of the Virgo cluster, and the luminous young quasar 3C273, may be cited as examples of celestial objects displaying solitary jets.) Upon occasion, an abrupt and more substantial ingestion of matter into a supermassive black hole - from one specific direction - must produce a strong ejection in the form of a single jet visible to optical telescopes. Drawn into the vicinity of a black hole abyss, the vast bulk of such mass-energy will be accelerated to escape velocity. After missing the exceedingly diminutive singularity itself, it will subsequently pass right through the region of the core and emerge from the opposite side as a powerful radiation/particle jet.

It would therefore appear as though a solution to the enigma of multiple radio sources and jets has its roots in a revised concept of gravitation - one in which it is conceded that *efficiency is linked to relative motion by the formula depicted in Figure #2.*

Appendix 3

Inferred Separation of Galactic Associations

Companion Systems	MILKY Way from Edge 10 MLY Separation (LY)	Milky Way from Edge 5 MLY Separation (LY)	Milky Way from Edge 3 MLY Separation (LY)	Milky Way from Edge 2 MLY Separation (LY)	Milky Way from Edge 1 MLY Separation (LY)
NGC7603	263,000	131,500	79,000	52,600	26,300
AM2006-295	696,000	348,000	209,000	139,200	69,600
NGC 1232	157,000	78,500	47,000	31,400	15,700
AM0328-222	577,000	288,500	173,000	115,400	57,700
AM059-4024	310,000	155,000	93,000	62,000	31,000
AM2054-221	1,107,000	553,500	332,000	221,400	110,700

Stephan's Quintet:

NGC7320 from NGC7318B	163,000	81,500	49,000	32,600	16,300
NGC7320 from R = 6,700 km/s Members	197,000	98,500	59,000	39,400	19,700
NGC7318B from R = 6,700 km/s Members	33,000	16,500	10,000	6,600	3,300

Appendix #4

Evolution of "M" Stages

Status or "Step"	Status "M" Stage	Quantity Individual Entities	Individual "A" Content	Number of Worlds	Quantity per World
309	Prior to Man	2×10^{27}	5×10^{92}	10^{22}	2×10^{5}
310	M^{1}	10^{27}	10^{93}	10^{17}	10^{10}
311	M^{2}	5×10^{26}	2×10^{93}	10^{17}	5×10^{9}
312	M^{3}	2.5×10^{26}	4×10^{93}	10^{17}	2.5×10^{9}
313	M^{4}	1.25×10^{26}	8×10^{93}	10^{17}	1.25×10^{9}
314	M^{5}	6.25×10^{25}	1.6×10^{94}	10^{17}	6.25×10^{8}
315	M^{6}	3.12×10^{25}	3.2×10^{94}	10^{17}	3.12×10^{8}
316	M^{7}	1.56×10^{25}	6.4×10^{94}	10^{17}	1.56×10^{8}
317	M^{8}	7.81×10^{24}	1.28×10^{95}	10^{17}	7.81×10^{7}
318	M^{9}	3.91×10^{24}	2.56×10^{95}	10^{17}	3.91×10^{7}
319	M^{10}	1.95×10^{24}	5.12×10^{95}	10^{17}	1.95×10^{7}
320	M^{11}	9.77×10^{23}	1.02×10^{96}	10^{17}	9.77×10^{6}
321	M^{12}	4.88×10^{23}	2.05×10^{96}	10^{17}	4.88×10^{6}
322	M^{13}	2.44×10^{23}	4.1×10^{96}	10^{17}	2.44×10^{6}
323	M^{14}	1.22×10^{23}	8.19×10^{96}	10^{17}	1.22×10^{6}
324	M^{15}	6.1×10^{22}	1.64×10^{97}	10^{17}	6.1×10^{5}
325	M^{16}	3.05×10^{22}	3.28×10^{97}	10^{17}	3.05×10^{5}
326	M^{17}	1.53×10^{22}	6.55×10^{97}	10^{17}	1.53×10^{5}
327	Stellar Black Hole	7.63×10^{21}	1.31×10^{98}	10^{22}	1

Appendix 5

Quasars Near Massive Galaxies

Strong statistical evidence exists in support of the concept of "galactic arcing," by which the aforementioned D/R factor is seen to be responsible for producing the illusion of a disproportionate number of quasars seemingly associated with massive galaxies. In order to achieve this clumping, in the angular distribution of quasars, it is necessary for these images to have been displaced from regions adjacent to such an intervening galactic source. Accordingly, it may be deduced that there must prevail a scenario whereby an overabundance of quasar images-in the immediate vicinity of a massive galaxy - is replaced by a shortage of images beyond a certain point, as the D/R factor acts to divert the course of approaching radiation.

Remarkable confirmation of this prediction may be found in the research of several astronomers,* in which a dearth of quasars is indeed shown to characterize the outlying regions surrounding massive galactic systems. Just as the phenomenon of "cosmic arcing" was revealed to displace images upon the large-scale, so the D/R factor is disclosed to produce the small-scale effect of "galactic arcing."

---

* Among the more astute scientists to pioneer this important line of research are Dr. Halton C. Arp and Dr. Geoffrey Burbidge, whose published works have inspired much controversy and cast doubt as to the credibility of many accepted views. (An informative account of such statistics is summarized in an article by David Cherry, entitled "Redshifts and the Spirit of Scientific Inquiry,"*21st Century Science & Technology,* May - June, 1989.)

Appendix 6

Supercluster Separations

Impressive evidence, confirming a Small Bang/Steady-state cosmology, may be found in a symmetrical "honeycomb" pattern which is now revealed in the distribution of galaxy superclusters. (See: "Large-scale distribution of galaxies at the Galactic poles," *Nature,* February 22, 1990.) Quite inexplicable in terms of any Big Bang creation, it is observed that remarkably periodic separations characterize the spatial arrangement of superclusters. This unexpected homogeneity is precisely what must be inferred upon the basis of our newly prescribed model! Indeed, not only is just such an overall pattern mandated, but there is also seen to be excellent agreement with regard to theoretical separations and the actual distance intervals measured in this recent deep-redshift survey. (The "Great Wall" feature, so described, is likely an effect of the phenomenon of "cosmic arcing.")

Appendix 7

Radiation Scattering and Cosmic Arcing

The phenomenon of "cosmic arcing" will be seen to have a rather subtle influence upon radiation with regard to observed luminosities. Since "repulsive" quanta are acknowledged to vary greatly in size or mass/energy content, it is to be expected that a proportion of interacting photons will be caused to diverge from a common trajectory - producing a degree of scattering which must be most pronounced with the increased "arcing" generally associated with very long transit times. In essence, the flux of radiation from objects of extremely high redshift (about z=4.00 and above, where considerable deflection is virtually assured) will be noticeably reduced due to lengthy and somewhat less than full homogeneity of encounters with the broad spectrum of "repulsive" quanta, resulting in a reduction of luminosity through scattering of many photons that would otherwise reach us. (This extreme redshift/luminosity effect was recently reported by a group of astronomers,* although it has been mistakenly attributed to increased opacity of the universe at an earlier stage of a Big Bang creation.)

* See: "Most Distant Quasar Probes Early Universe," *Astronomy,* March 1990 (page 10).

Appendix 8

The "Great Attractor"

Recent observation has raised the specter of an apparent contradiction with regard to the prescribed D/R formula. Dubbed the "Great Attractor" * by astronomers, this phenomenon would appear to discredit the prediction that gravitational attraction is converted to repulsion at distances exceeding about 17 MLY. A survey of more than 100 spiral galaxies (in our galactic neighborhood) reveals a streaming - at higher velocities that anticipated from Hubble's law - toward the general direction of the Hydra-Centaurus supercluster. This has been interpreted as an indication that some tens of thousands of largely unseen galaxies are exerting their gravitational pull across a distance of at least 150 MLY. Seeming to lend credence to this view is evidence that, at distances beyond this alleged "Great Attractor," there is a slight reduction of redshift (from normal Hubble flow) which would imply an "infalling" toward this theorized supermassive influence.

What must be considered, however, is the effect of "cosmic arcing" upon radiation propagating in the immediate vicinity of the cosmic edge. Since a relatively small difference in a galaxy's proximity to the edge can have a magnified effect upon redshift, it could cause one system to appear more remote than another that - due to greater angular distance - is actually further from the Milky Way. Hence, it is possible for some galaxies to exhibit higher redshifts than others that are more remote! The "infalling" illusion is also seen to have a most logical explanation, merely requiring a certain relative orientation - at time of light emission - to produce the observed effect.

Thus, by reason of our highly eccentric cosmic location, we are permitted to glimpse displacement/distortion of celestial images upon a scale of the order of our own supercluster. It may well be said that the "Great Attractor" should really be called the "Great Illusion."

* See: "Great Attractor Confirmed," *Sky & Telescope,* May, 1990 (pages 475-476).